Happy Horsemanship

Happy Horsemanship

by

Dorothy Henderson Pinch

Illustrated by the author

VAN NOSTRAND REINHOLD COMPANY

New York   Cincinnati   Toronto   London   Melbourne

VAN NOSTRAND REINHOLD COMPANY REGIONAL OFFICES:
New York Cincinnati Chicago Millbrae Dallas

VAN NOSTRAND REINHOLD COMPANY FOREIGN OFFICES:
London Toronto Melbourne

Published by VAN NOSTRAND REINHOLD COMPANY
450 West 33rd Street, New York, N.Y. 10001

Published simultaneously in Canada by
D. VAN NOSTRAND COMPANY (Canada), LTD.

16 15 14 13 12 11 10 9 8 7 6 5 4 3 2

Contents

1. To Introduce Myself

Horses are . . .

something to dream about . . .

and to wish for;

fun to watch . . .

and to make friends with;

nice to pat . . .

and great to hug;

5

and oh, what a joy to ride!

For you to enjoy me (and for me to enjoy you, too) there are some important facts about me which you should know before you try to handle or ride me.

I am a HORSE.

My name in Latin is *Equus*. From this name comes the word "equine," which means something to do with a horse, and the word "equestrian," which means one who rides a horse.

My name in Greek is *Hippos*. From this name come the words "hippocampus," the sea horse, and "hippopotamus," the river horse, and also "hippophile," the lover of horses. (I hope you are a hippophile!)

I am a *mammal*, which means I feed my young with milk. My baby is called a *foal*. It is said to be *foaled* when it is born. A foal becomes a *weanling* from the time it leaves its mother until it is a year old, at which time it is known as a *yearling*. (A Thoroughbred horse's birthday is considered to be the first of January, no matter on what date it was foaled.)

A male horse is called a *colt* until three years of age. Then he becomes a *stallion,* unless altered to make him more tractable, in which case he is called a *gelding.*

The female horse is called a *mare* and she is known as a *filly* until three years of age.

The mother of a foal is its *dam*, its father is called its *sire*. A foal is said to be "out of" its dam and "by" its sire.

7

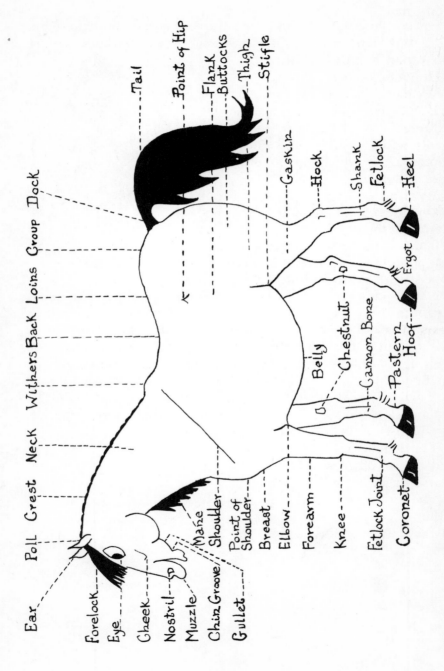

Here are the correct names for the parts of my body.

Now let me tell you some things you should know about my body.

When you talk about it, you can divide it into three parts: the *forehand,* the *barrel,* and the *hindquarters.* The forehand includes the head, neck, shoulders, withers, forelegs. The barrel is composed of the back, ribs and belly. The hindquarters include the loins, flank, croup, tail, buttocks and hindlegs.

My left side is called the *near* side and my right side the *off* side.

I am a *vertebrate*—I have a backbone.

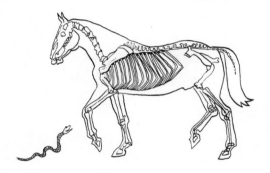

My height is measured from the ground to the highest point of my backbone at the withers. All horses are measured in *hands;* one hand equals four inches. Any horse measuring 14 hands, 2 inches, or less is known as a *pony.* (Some of the larger breeds of horses grow to be as much as 18 hands in height!)

I am a *quadruped*—which means that I have four feet.

My front legs are called *forelegs*. They bend at the *elbow, knee, fetlock,* and *pastern* joints. They carry most of my weight but do not need to be rested as often as my back legs do. Above the knee, on the inside of my foreleg, is a small, horny growth, called a *chestnut* or *castor*. The hair on the fetlock grows long, to carry moisture of sweat and rain away from my heel. *Watch out for your toes when I am stamping my forelegs to free them from flies in the summer!*

My back legs are called my *hindlegs*. I push or propel my body with my hindlegs. When sleeping or relaxing, I rest one hindleg at a time.

My hindlegs bend at the *stifle, hock, fetlock,* and *pastern joints*. There is a *chestnut* on the inside of each hindleg. When startled, I use my hind legs to protect myself, by kicking. Do not stand or walk near my hindlegs—*you might be kicked!*

My eyes look forward. I have to turn my head in order to see behind me. My eyes should be large, bright and set far apart.

My ears can move separately, forward and backward. Sometimes my ears, like your eyebrows, can reveal my state of mind. If you watch my ears, you can often know my humor. When both ears are forward—I am cheerful, interested, and alert. When they move backward and forward—I am alert and listening for your voice. When I am relaxing or dozing, my ears usually hang *toward the side*. (Some horses' ears are naturally set in this manner. They are said to be *lop-eared*.)

When both ears go back, watch out! I am displeased! This is like your frown. The more my ears turn back the more I am scowling! When you see my ears go back, try to find the reason for my anger or irritation. Always be *very* careful around my teeth and heels when my ears are pinned back!

My forehead should be broad and flat. This usually means that I am sensible and agreeable. (A narrow forehead and a bulging skull between the eyes often denotes a mean and excitable nature.)

The upper lip of my *muzzle* is strong and elastic. It stretches out to pull grass and hay into my mouth. (Be sure it does not accidentally pull your fingers between my teeth when you are feeding me a tidbit.) (When I am sleepy or tired, or getting old, sometimes my lower lip relaxes and hangs down.)

During my lifetime I have two sets of teeth. My age until six can be determined by the growth or loss of my first or "milk" teeth. After six the appearance, shape, and degree of wear on my front teeth give information about my age. Until I am nine years old my age is given like yours, but after that I am said to be *aged*. Mares have thirty-six permanent teeth but stallions or geldings have four extra teeth called *tushes*. It is important for you to understand the way my jaw is made if you want to have control over me. I respond to the *bit* in my mouth because when you pull on the reins it puts pressure on a very sensitive part of my jaw, called the *bars*.

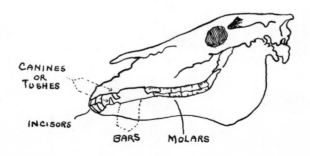

CANINES OR TUSHES

INCISORS

BARS   MOLARS

The *bars* are the toothless area in the lower jaw, between the front, or *incisor,* teeth and the back, or *molar,* teeth. Different pressures on these bars by the bit will cause me to turn, raise or lower my head, relax my jaw and *flex* at the *poll.* Much of your control of my direction, gaits, speed and balance comes from properly applied pressures to the bars of my jaw. The pressure of your finger or thumb against these bars will cause me to open my mouth for the bit, with no danger to your hand. Be careful not to put your fingers accidentally between my teeth instead of my bars!

I have a long flexible neck. I can bend it around so I can see behind me. Its length is useful in reaching far back on my sides to chase flies or scratch itches. Very handy! I can also bend it around so I can nip the unwary while I am being groomed or saddled! (Fastening me with a short rope or on *cross-tie ropes* may help prevent an unpleasant surprise!)

Beause my neck is long and flexible it is easy for me to reach the ground to eat grass. This is called *grazing*. (Sometimes I try to graze while you are riding me, which I should not do! Do not try to outpull me to raise my head—you may lose and be pulled over my head by the reins! Use your legs against my sides, and send me forward, then I have to raise my head whether I want to or not.)

I use my neck in different ways to help keep my whole body in balance. The position of my neck affects my body balance, the height I raise my legs and the length of my stride—I stretch out my neck for speed, and raise and bend it for high-stepping paces. And sometimes I use the position of my neck to avoid the controlling action of the bit! *For best control, my neck should be kept straight in front of my body*.

On the top of my neck grows long, coarse hair, called my *mane*. The hair which grows between my ears and hangs over my forehead is called my *forelock*.

My mane usually is trained to hang on the right hand side of my neck.

A cow pony's mane is trained to fall on the left side of his neck, so that it will not interfere with the cowboy's use of his rope on the right side. A polo pony's mane is clipped off close to the neck, so it will not be in the way of the polo player's mallet. This is called a *clipped, roached* or *hogged* mane.

For special occasions and horse shows, manes are often plaited in braids, sometimes with colored ribbon or yarn added, to make a more attractive appearance. When the mane is thinned by pulling out some of the hairs, or is made even or shortened by breaking off uneven strands, it is said to be *pulled*.

15

My foot is called a *hoof*.

The outside covering of my hoof is hard and horny. The top of the hoof, where the flesh of the leg changes to the horn of the hoof, is called the *coronet*. The wedge-shaped pad of elastic tissue in the sole of my hoof is called the *frog*. The frog serves as a shock absorber. To protect my hoof from wearing down or

PARTS OF HOOF

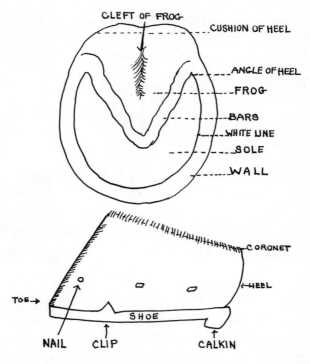

splitting, a steel *horseshoe* is nailed to its edges. (This is not painful, since the outside of my hoof has no more feeling than your fingernail.)

To make it fit my hoof, the shoe is heated with fire in a *forge* and then hammered into shape on an *anvil*. These shoes must be removed and the new growth trimmed from my hooves every five or six weeks. Then my shoes are said to be *pulled* and *reset*.

I am *shod* by a man called a *farrier* or *blacksmith*. His workshop is known as a *smithy*.

17

The angle of my shoulder makes a difference in the length of my stride. A sloping shoulder is best if I am to be used for riding. Good depth through the front of my body gives plenty of space for my lungs. My lungs need room to expand when I am going at speed. I am said to have good *wind* when nothing interferes with my breathing. A good spring of ribs provides plenty of room for my digestive organs. If my ribs are short and flat I will not be able to digest and use my food as well. I will not be as easy to keep in good condition nor will I have the stamina of a horse with a large spring of rib.

A short, strong back helps me carry your weight easily, and muscular hindquarters propel me with the least effort.

The hair of my tail is usually the same color as my mane. This hair grows from the top of my *dock*. The thickness and length varies from the scant and often too short tail of the Appaloosa to the long, luxurious tail of the Shetland pony.

My tail is very useful in the summertime to keep my body brushed free of flies.

My tail is sometimes braided down the dock when I am being shown in horse shows. If my tail has been shortened, as was formerly done with driving horses, it is said to be *docked*.

When I am feeling lively I carry my tail high.

My body is covered with hair of varying length and thickness, called my *coat*. My coat grows from my head toward my tail. The length and thickness of this coat changes twice a year, in the spring and autumn. For winter I grow a dense *undercoat,* which insulates me against the cold, with coarse longer or *guard* hairs, which shed rain and give added protection against wind and snow.

In the spring this heavy coat falls out (which is called *shedding*) and I grow a short, fine summer coat. The thickness of my winter coat depends a great deal on the climate of the country in which my ancestors lived. For example, ponies from the northern countries of Shetland Isles and Wales grow much heavier and longer winter coats than do horses like the Thoroughbred with their Arab, Turk and Barb southern ancestry.

If I am to be ridden fast after my winter coat is grown, the hair is usually clipped from my body so I will not become overheated. For foxhunting the long hair is left on my legs to protect against bushes and briars, and sometimes it is also left under the saddle to prevent chafing.

When I am healthy my coat is soft and shiny. A dull, rough coat is a sign of poor condition. Regular grooming makes me look sleek and feel well.

2. How I Behave

I *am* a horse, so naturally, I behave like one. In general I am a friendly animal, and I usually like people very much. I like to be patted and talked to. But if you pat my head, please keep your hand below my eyes. The best place to pat is my neck or shoulder. These are a safe distance from my teeth and heels, and I can see where you are.

Approach me from the front where I can see you easily. Speak to me in a quiet, reassuring voice.

Don't surprise me by running at me, or shouting loudly.

If you must approach me from the rear, use your voice to let me know that you are coming. (Otherwise I might kick first and look second!)

I like to be given tidbits like sugar, or carrots, or apples. But don't try to feed me when I have a bit in my mouth, for this makes it difficult for me to chew. Wait until my work is done to reward me.

Always present these "goodies" on the flat of your palm with fingers extended. (If your fingers are curled, I might accidentally nip them while nibbling the tidbit!)

We horses have ticklish spots—just as you do. If you touch or brush these spots we act as you would—we try to get away, or somehow stop the person from annoying us. Horses cannot say, "Stop it, I'm ticklish!" So they nip or kick to show their annoyance. The side behind the elbow is often a ticklish area. (For this reason many horses try to nip when their saddles are tightened.)

The flank in front of the hip is another spot that is often quite sensitive. Horses sometimes kick forward, or "cowkick," when touched or brushed there. Be careful around ticklish spots!

I am a herd animal. In my natural state I travel in groups.

By choice I stay with other horses. When I am separated from my friends I may try to go back—or join other horses . . .

or even to return to my stable or another stable. So don't be surprised if I do not willingly leave another horse. It may take a bit of persuasion on your part!

Any time I see other horses running, I may become excited and start to run, too! (So give me a soothing word!) When I am being ridden with other horses, if they go faster I will try to keep up with them—or maybe even pass them! (Sometimes I get very annoyed if I am kept behind. Don't try to outpull me —let me go in front or take me far away from the group. Then I won't be so anxious to run.)

Even when I am being ridden alone there are moments when I want to hurry—especially when I know that I am going toward my stable!

My conduct can be most disturbing if I lag behind other horses and suddenly decide to hurry and join them. In my enthusiasm I often playfully buck and kick, just as if I were running free in pasture. So don't let me get into a spot where I will feel that I should hurry to catch up with the group. (If I do, tighten your seat in the saddle and don't let me lower my head. For a really good, unseating buck I have to put my head down!)

I am a rather timid animal.
When I see something new and strange, I may be frightened.

When something frightens me I may try to run away from it; be prepared to calm and control me when I am afraid.

I jump away from sights and sounds that seem threatening to me. This is called *shying*. Be sure to sit securely in the saddle—if I am startled, I may move quickly and unseat you!

Loud and sudden noises may cause me to run away from them—use a soothing voice and a steadying hand to calm me.

31

Although generally I like other horses, sometimes I *don't* like one in particular, and I may try to start a fight. And, just like you, I sometimes quarrel with my playmates. We horses often start a fuss when we get our heads together, so *don't* let us touch noses!

Sometimes I may kick at other horses, and they at me; so when riding, keep your horse well away from other horses' heels!

Changes in weather change my behavior. When I hear and feel the wind blowing I may become very lively. (If you want me to stand on a windy day, turn my tail toward the wind so my chest will not be chilled.)

Except on cold and windy days, rain does not affect me. It takes a heavy rainfall, or rain driven by a strong wind, to penetrate my protective hair coat. Then I may be chilled. (If I am rainsoaked I will dry quickly, without chilling, if you cover me with a thin, all wool cover called a *cooler*.)

On warm days I may be sleepy. If I am dozing in the sunshine, be sure to speak to me as you approach, so that I will not be startled by your presence. I may even be lazy when ridden, for I am usually much calmer and move more slowly on a warm day than I do on a cold one.

Never leave me tied out in the sun on a hot day; always tie me in the cool shade. Be sure that my pasture has some protection from the direct rays of the sun, either shade trees or a shed.

On cold days I am usually much more lively than at any other time. Especially when I come out of a warm barn on a cold day I may feel *very* frisky. Start directing my energies right away on a cold day—vigorous trotting is best. (It is easier for me to buck or kick from a cantering stride than from a trot. Holding me down to a walk just bottles up my steam—which may explode later!)

I can talk to you or other horses only by *neighing* or *whinnying*. This is the sound I make for greeting and pleasure, and sometimes for excitement or fear. When I am lonely I whinny for other horses. Take heed if I whinny while I am being ridden; if I am lonesome, I may try to return to my stable or join other horses!

Since I have a good appetite and like greenery, I may try to snatch at branches and bushes while I am being ridden. Don't let me! When I am being ridden I should pay attention to what I am doing, and not be distracted by things which I find interesting. Never let me eat with a bit in my mouth; I can't chew properly anyway, and I am sure to get my bit dirty.

Try to understand and remember how I may behave under certain conditions. Knowing what to expect of me can keep both of us out of trouble, and assure an enjoyable ride for us both.

3. Let's Get Ready!

Always approach me from my near (left) side, if you can. This is the side from which I am led, tacked and untacked, and mounted and dismounted, as well. Always walk (don't run!) quietly toward me. It is better to move toward my neck, rather than go directly to my head. (Sometimes I will jump away if a hand is suddenly raised to my face.)

It is always wise to say a few words to me as you approach from any direction. A kind but firm voice will tell me that you are a friend that I can trust; I might be frightened or upset by a loud, rough voice. It is *most* important to speak to me if you must approach me from the rear. When I hear your voice I will know that you are coming, but otherwise I might be startled and kick first, then look around afterwards.

Don't put a hand unexpectedly upon my hindquarters! I may be surprised, and kick. Anytime it is necessary to touch my hindquarters, put your hand on my neck or shoulder first, and move it slowly back over my body, speaking to me at the same time. Then I will know what is touching me and will not be surprised or frightened.

If you need to go from one side of me to the other, pass in front of me or under my neck, if possible. Otherwise, go far enough behind me to be well out of reach of my heels.

When I am loose in my *stall*, which is my room in the *stable*, or out to eat grass in my *pasture*, I usually wear a *halter*, with which I can be led or tied. Sometimes it is hung outside my stall, ready for use. The proper piece of equipment with which to lead me is called a *leadshank*. As I like to chew on leather, the part near my mouth is made of chain links—which spoils all my fun! Lead me from my near side, walking by my head or with me a little behind you.

Don't let me get in front of you or with my head turned toward the right. In either of these positions I can be difficult to control and may even get away from you! Hold the leadshank in your right hand about six inches from my head. Be sure not to let the extra length dangle on the ground, where it might be trampled or tangled around your legs! Fold the loose end in the palm of your left hand. (Never wrap it around your hand—if I started to run, you would be caught and dragged after me!)

When leading me, look in the direction in which you are going and walk forward; usually I will come with you without any urging. If I do not start immediately, or lag back, don't try to pull me after you. I can—and will—outpull you anytime! Bring me forward with little tugs on the leadshank; I don't resist that kind of pressure. Do not look back at me except when you lead me through narrow places, such as gates or doorways. Then always watch carefully that I enter the opening straight and do not strike my hips. (The point of my hip is like your elbow—the bone is right under the skin with no flesh to protect it, so if it strikes a post or doorjamb I can be painfully injured. Ouch!)

To steer me while leading: a tug on the leadshank will direct my head toward the left, the firm pressure of your shoulder or elbow against my neck will move me toward the right. To slow down or stop—again, short tugs instead of a steady pull. And always remember to let me know what you want. (A firm, commanding "whoa!" will mean "stop!" to me.)

Always *groom* me before I am ridden. Grooming is the way you keep me clean. These are the tools used for this purpose. Together they are called my *grooming kit*. Put my grooming kit in a box or basket with a handle. This makes it easy to carry and store the tools.

The *hoof pick*—for cleaning out the feet.

The *dandy brush*—for removing heavy dirt, caked mud and sweat from my coat.

The *body brush*—to remove dust and scurf from coat, mane and tail.

The *curry comb*—for cleaning the body brush.

The *water brush*—to use damp, on mane, tail, legs and feet.

The *stable sponge*—for cleaning eyes, nostrils, lips, dock and body bathing.

The *stable rubber*—for a final polish after grooming.

The *sweat scraper*—to remove sweat and water from the coat.

HOOF PICK DANDY BRUSH

BODY BRUSH CURRY COMB

WATER BRUSH SPONGE

STABLE RUBBER SWEAT SCRAPER

When you are ready to groom me bring my grooming kit, and a bucket of water as well. Fasten me by my halter with a rope that is short enough to keep me from reaching around and nipping you. Remember I have ticklish spots, and if I am touched on one of these places while you are grooming me, the only way I can show my annoyance is by a nip or a kick. Behind the elbows, under the belly and the flank in front of the hip may be sensitive spots, so brush carefully and watch my teeth and heels!

Pick up each hoof in turn; remove whatever may be lodged in the foot with the point of the hoof pick, working downward from heel to toe.

Now the dandy brush may be used, beginning at the poll on the near side and working toward the tail. This stiff, long-bristled brush may be used in either hand in short, sweeping motions, drawn briskly through the hair. It is especially useful for removing sweat marks from the saddle region, and caked dirt from the belly and points of the hocks, fetlocks and pasterns. (It is best not to use this stiff brush on the more tender parts of my body.) When working on my hindlegs, hold my tail in your free hand. (This often discourages me from kicking.)

Next, use the body brush to groom my entire body. Its soft bristles are used in short, circular strokes in the direction of the lay of my coat. It can be used comfortably on my entire body, including my head.

The hand nearest the head holds the body brush, and the curry comb is held in the other hand. After four or five strokes, draw the brush smartly across the teeth of the curry comb to dislodge the dirt. (The curry comb is cleaned by tapping it on the floor.)

To do my mane, first throw it over the wrong side of my neck and brush the crest. Bring it back to the right side and brush a few locks at a time. Brush the ends first to remove the tangles, then work toward the roots.

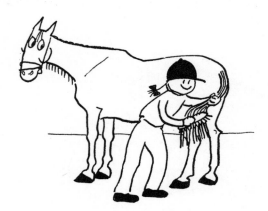

My tail is cared for in the same manner. Hold the tail to one side (*don't* stand *behind* me!) and shake out a few locks at a time. Your hand firmly holding the hair between my dock and the tangle you are unsnarling spares me any discomfort.

The sponge cleanses my eyes, nostrils, lips and under my dock. (It is used also to bathe the sweat from under my saddle and bridle after I have been ridden on a warm day or to bathe my entire body if I have become overheated in the hot weather. Tepid water, with liniment added, is used for this bathing.)

The sweat scraper is drawn over the coat in the direction of hair growth to free it of sweat or wash water.

The soft end hairs of the water brush, dipped in a bucket with the excess water squeezed out against the edge, are used to dampen my mane and keep it smooth. Start at the roots and brush downward. This brush may be used to put a finishing touch on the top of my tail and legs, as well.

Last of all use the stable rubber, folded, to polish my coat after the cleansing tools have been used. Now I am spic and span—and ready to be saddled.

When you ride me I wear a *bridle*, a *saddle* and sometimes a *martingale*. Together these are called my *tack*, just as your coat, hat, shoes, etc. are called your clothes. They are kept in a *tackroom*. I am said to be *tacked up* or *untacked*.

My bridle and martingale help you to manage me. My saddle makes it easier for you to stay on my back, and a lot more comfortable, too! A bridle is made of leather, with a metal *bit*. I wear the bridle on my head, with the bit in my mouth. The *reins*, which you will be holding in your hands, are attached to this bit, so through them you can create different pressures on the sensitive bars of my jaw.

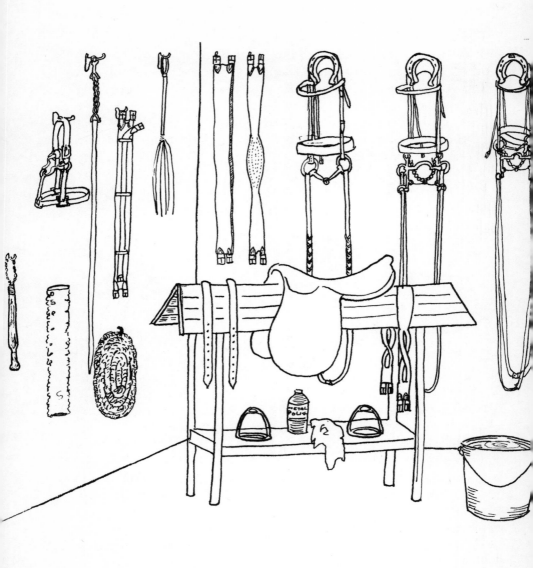

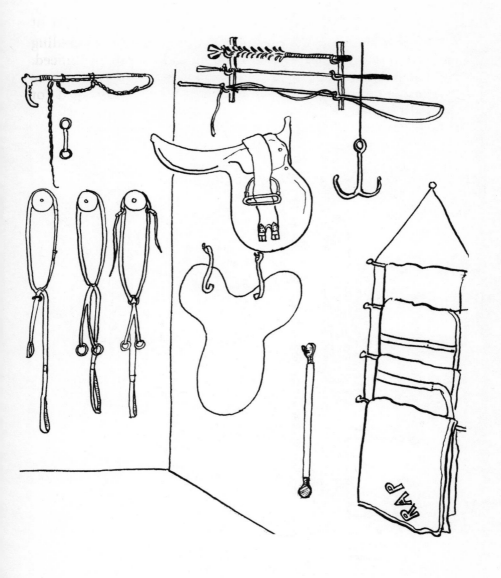

The proper use of *bit pressures* is a very important part of your control over me. This will be an aid to you in guiding and balancing me, and in changing my gaits and rates of speed.

A bridle takes its name from the bit attached to it. The three types illustrated below are the ones most commonly used for riding. Each bit serves a different purpose of control.

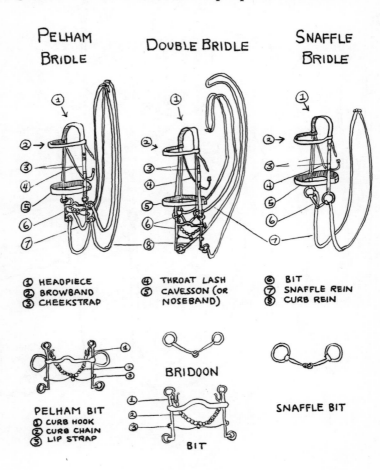

PELHAM BRIDLE

DOUBLE BRIDLE

SNAFFLE BRIDLE

① HEADPIECE
② BROWBAND
③ CHEEKSTRAP
④ THROAT LASH
⑤ CAVESSON (OR NOSEBAND)
⑥ BIT
⑦ SNAFFLE REIN
⑧ CURB REIN

PELHAM BIT
❶ CURB HOOK
❷ CURB CHAIN
❸ LIP STRAP

BRIDOON

BIT

SNAFFLE BIT

When carrying my bridle from the tackroom, hang its headpiece over your left forearm with the browband toward your elbow. Be sure to have the reins hung evenly on your arm—don't drag them in the dust! Unfasten my halter, keeping a firm grip on the strap; slip it over my muzzle  and refasten it around my neck. (This will free my head for the bridle but I will still be securely tied.)

Stand by my head, facing in the same direction I do, and put the reins over my head. Next, put your right hand under my jaw and up around the other side to the center of my face, just above my nostrils. Take the center of both cheekpieces in this hand, which then can be used to keep my head down if I try to raise it away from the bit. (I often do try it—wouldn't you?)

If you spread the bit between thumb and forefinger of your left hand and gently press it against my teeth where they join—never shove it up under my lip, like some people do!—I will usually open my mouth and cheerfully accept the bit. If I don't, the pressure of one of your bent fingers on the toothless bars of my lower jaw will cause me to open my mouth and receive the bit. There is no danger of being nipped there, but don't accidentally put your fingers between my front teeth!

Guide the bit into my mouth with your left hand, drawing it into position by raising the cheekpieces with your right hand. The left hand can now assist the right to put the headpiece over each ear in turn. (It doesn't hurt my ears to be bent forward gently.) Then be sure to smooth my mane and forelock under the headpiece. Next, fasten the throat lash loosely—otherwise it will interfere with my breathing. The width of your hand should fit between it and my jaw bone.

Check my bridle's fit by standing in front of me, making sure that my browband is straight (not pushed up pinching my ears) and that the cavesson (noseband) is even, halfway between the points of my cheekbones and the corners of my lips. In this position it will neither rub my cheekbones nor pinch the corners of my lips. The ends of all straps should be through the loops sewn close to the buckles, called *keepers,* and the sliding loops, called *runners.* (Loose strap ends are very untidy.)

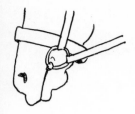 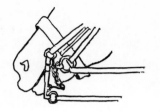 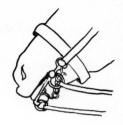

The *snaffle* bit should hang so it just wrinkles the corners of my lips. The *bridoon* of the double bridle hangs in the same position, with the *bit* just below and in front of it. A *Pelham* bit is hung to touch the corners of my lips. The links of the *curb chain* should be turned until it lies smoothly in my chin groove.

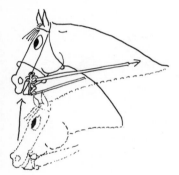 

The snaffle bit acts upon the bars of my jaw and the corners of my lips. It is used to raise and turn my head.

The *curb* bit acts only on the bars of the jaw. (The curb chain in the chin groove gives leverage and increases the pressure on my jaw.) The curb bit is used to lower my head and to flex my neck, by making me relax my poll. (In a pelham bit the snaffle and curb reins should never be tightened at the same time.)

51

Sometimes I learn that if I raise my head beyond a certain point it becomes difficult for you to manage me. If I do, use a martingale to limit the height to which I can raise my head. (The bit won't press the place in my mouth that makes me pay attention if my head is too high and my nose is up in the air.) If I am to wear a martingale, it is placed around my shoulders before I am bridled.

A *standing martingale* is a strap attached to the cavesson at one end and to the girth at the other, passing through a slot in the neckpiece. (To check for correct length, put your hand underneath and push up; it should just reach into my gullet.)

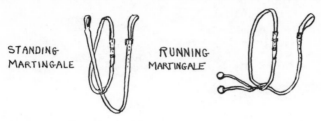

STANDING MARTINGALE

RUNNING MARTINGALE

The *running martingale* is also attached to the girth, with the other end dividing into two straps, each with a ring at the end, through which my snaffle or curb reins are passed. (The usual measurement for this martingale is to reach my withers with both rings held on one side.)

The neckstrap of both martingales should buckle on the left side and be loose enough to admit the width of your hand at my withers. A properly fitted martingale can prevent me from playing tricks on you!

These are the Parts of my _SADDLE_

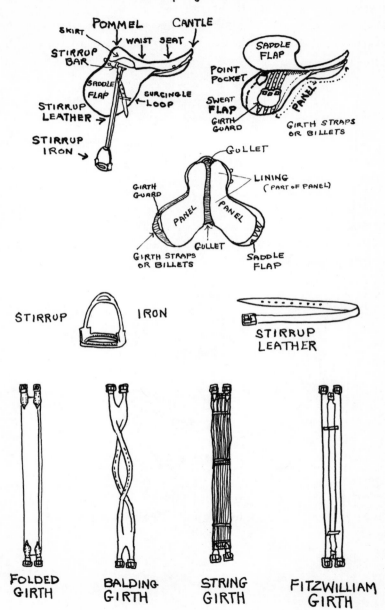

STIRRUP IRON

STIRRUP LEATHER

FOLDED GIRTH

BALDING GIRTH

STRING GIRTH

FITZWILLIAM GIRTH

Now I am ready to be saddled. Carry my saddle from the tackroom on your left forearm, the *pommel* (front end) toward your elbow, and with your right hand under the *cantle* (back end).

Place the saddle lightly over my withers. (Don't slam it down!) Slide it back into position in the hollows behind my shoulders. (This will smooth the hair under the saddle in the direction of growth. Matting the hair by pushing the saddle forward against my coat may cause a saddle sore!) Always be sure that the saddle is set far enough behind my shoulder blades for it to not interfere with their free movement. A saddle set too far forward also puts the girth too close to my elbows, pinching my skin and giving me a girth gall.

After the saddle is set properly on my back, see that all is flat and smooth under the *saddle flap*. Go quietly around the front or under my neck to the off side. Check that all is flat and smooth under this flap and let down the *girth*. Now back to the near side, and keeping your shoulder close to mine and facing toward my tail, bend down and take hold of the girth. If I am wearing a martingale, slip the girth through the martingale loop. Then buckle the girth. Do this one hole at a time, and DON'T try to do it all in one big pull! It hurts! If after the girth has been drawn up snugly there is just enough room to admit your hand between the girth and my body, the saddle will be secure and I will be comfortable, too.

Slide the four fingers of your left hand under the girth just below the saddle flap and draw them slowly down my body under my belly, to smooth out any wrinkles formed in my skin by the tightening of the girth. These wrinkles in front of the girth cause me great discomfort and often create sores. Sometimes I hold my breath when you start to tighten the girth, which makes my body larger than it will be when I am ridden.

Always check your girth before mounting to be sure it has not become too slack after I have let out my breath.

4. How to Get On and Off

When you are ready to *mount,* unbuckle the halter which has been fastened around my neck. (Be sure to hang it on a convenient hook. Don't just drop it on the ground!)

Grasp both snaffle reins three or four inches below my chin and lead me around a minute or two before mounting. (This settles the saddle comfortably upon my back and makes me exhale any breath which I might have been holding in order to keep you from tightening up my girth.)

Then stand with your left shoulder close to my near shoulder, and slide your left arm through the rein on that side. (This frees both your hands for use but still keeps control over me.)

Now check the girth to see if it can be tightened a hole or two. Never mount until you have made certain that your saddle is secure. (Otherwise you may end up on the wrong side of your horse—the bottom, not the top!)

Also, it is always wise to measure the stirrup leathers on a saddle before mounting, because the person who last rode the saddle might have had legs much shorter than yours, or much longer! (If you don't measure and make any necessary changes before mounting, you may find yourself in a very awkward predicament!)

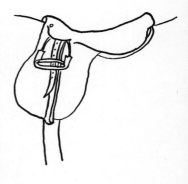

You will find that the stirrup irons on my saddle have been secured so they will not catch on things or hit my sides while I am being led. (If they are left dangling they could give you a very nasty blow on the head when I am being untacked!) This is done by running the iron up to the stirrup bar on the leather next to the saddle, then tucking the leather down through the iron.

Draw the leather out of the iron and, grasping the bottom of the iron in your left hand, pull it down to the bottom of the leather. Extend your right arm until its fingertips touch the stirrup bar, then draw the iron and the leather along the bottom surface of this outstretched arm. If the  bottom of the iron touches your body at the armpit, the length of this leather will be very close to the correct measurement for you.

If not exactly the right length, it will be near enough for you to be secure and comfortable during and after mounting. An adjustment of a hole or two can be made after you are seated in the saddle. Shortening and lengthening the stirrup leather is more easily managed if the buckle is drawn down to the middle of the saddle flap. (A tug on the end of the leather will bring the buckle into a convenient position.) After changing the length of the leather, don't forget to pull the part of the leather next to the saddle, to return the buckle to its proper place under the protecting skirt. An exposed buckle would be very painful against your leg!

To check the length of the leather on the off side, keep your right hand on my left rein as you pass in front of me. Grasp my right rein in your left hand before letting go of my left rein. Then slide your right arm through the right rein. To again free your hands, let go with your left hand and measure the leather as you did on the nearside. After adjusting the leather, return to my near side and stand facing my hindquarters with your left shoulder close to mine. With the girth and leathers checked, all is in order to mount.

The next (and very important) thing to do is to adjust the reins so that you can control me while you are mounting. If you fail to do this, and I decide to move off when you are half on and half off, the results can be annoying and possibly even dangerous to you. To have this control, the reins should be held in your left hand, which rests on my withers but keeps a light, feeling *contact* with my mouth. (You will keep this contact with my mouth at all times when you ride me.) A slight movement backward of your hand would check me if I tried to step forward. (Of course, if the reins were not even, I would turn in the direction of the shorter rein and walk about in a circle. If I am inclined to turn around and take a nip at you, it may be necessary to shorten my right rein a trifle in self-defense!)

It is easy to get the reins even, as a buckle marks the middle of the snaffle reins and the curb reins are sewn together at the center. Take the buckle (and the center of the curb rein, if used) in your right hand and draw the reins through your left hand, which makes a little bridge over my withers. When you can lightly feel the bit in my mouth, you will have made contact, with the reins even. The extra end of the reins, called the *bight,* is dropped over my right shoulder, where it will not interfere with your mounting.

Your left hand may be used to help pull you up into the saddle by being placed over my withers or by grasping a piece of my mane. (This is not painful to me—it is like picking up a puppy by the nape of the neck.) It is not a good idea to take hold of the pommel of the saddle for this purpose. It drags uncomfortably on my backbone and, if my withers are flat, may cause the saddle to turn. Grasp the back of the stirrup iron in your right hand, and, turning it toward you, insert your left foot. Then, depending upon how tall I am in relation to you, move your right hand to the waist, cantle or flap of my saddle, to help you in mounting.

Spring from your right foot, pivoting your left foot toward the front. As your right leg swings over my hindquarters (be sure to clear them!) move your right hand to the front of the saddle.

Don't thump down into the saddle! Ease your weight down *gently*. (I won't have a very good opinion of you if you start off by banging down on my back! My kidneys are under the cantle and could be bruised.) Quietly slide your right foot into the offside stirrup iron. After settling in your saddle, you can check the measurement of your stirrup leathers by removing both feet from the irons—for a correct length, the bottom of the iron should be even with the middle of your ankle joint. DON'T mount from this position—

If I am kicking at a fly, I might accidentally kick you. If I were annoyed and meant to kick at you, I couldn't miss!

If I moved forward, you would be left dangling, and you could be dragged and badly hurt. Don't let this happen! Don't be careless!

If you mount from this position you are safely out of reach of my kicking hooves.

From this position if I move forward you can still swing into the saddle.

When you are ready to *dismount,* hold the reins together in your left hand, place it on my withers and put your right hand on the front of the saddle. (Don't put your fingers under the pommel—they might be pinched.) Remove your right foot from the stirrup iron, and with your weight on your stiffened arms, swing your right leg over and next to your left leg. As the right leg clears my hindquarters, move your right hand back to the cantle to support your weight. Now raise yourself on your stiffened arms just enough to free your left foot from the iron and slide to the ground, keeping your body close to the saddle and landing with both feet well under you.

Once on the ground, turn to face my tail, slide your left arm through the rein to free your hands and run up the stirrup iron on its leather. Then go around to the off side to run up the right iron. Return to my near side and hold me by standing opposite my head, with both reins in your right hand.

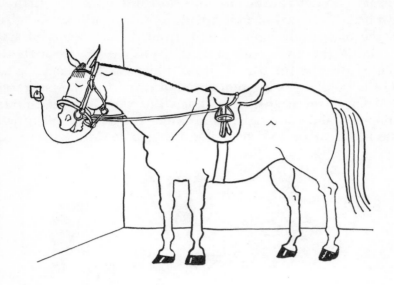

If you intend to ride me again and only want to tie me up for the time being, put my halter over my bridle and fasten the tie rope to the halter. Never fasten me by the bit in my bridle. If I get restless the pull of the rope on the bit in my mouth might make me try to rid myself of the discomfort by pulling back and breaking my bridle. (You would have damaged an expensive piece of equipment and I would be loose. You don't want either of these things to happen.)

When you tie me up with my tack on, place the buckle of my reins in the center of the saddle and tuck the left rein under the run-up stirrup iron. This will prevent the reins from slipping down if I lower my head. If the reins are loose, they can become tangled around my front legs, and might be broken in my efforts to free myself.

If it is time to untack me, remove my saddle, standing by my near shoulder (facing my tail) and unbuckle the girth. If I have been wearing a martingale, lean down and free the girth from the martingale loop. Pass in front of me to the off side, and folding the girth back on itself, push it up through the center of the run-up stirrup iron. This will keep it in place while the saddle is being removed and carried to the tackroom.

Go back to the near-side shoulder. Put your left hand under the pommel and your right hand under the cantle, and lift the saddle up, clear of my back; then bring it toward you.

Don't drag the saddle across my backbone instead of lifting it off first. This can be very painful to me!

Carry the saddle back to the tackroom the same way you brought it to me, and put it on its rack with the pommel towards the wall.

To remove my bridle, bring the reins (and the neckpiece of the martingale if there is one) forward to behind my ears, and refasten the halter around my neck. Stand by my neck on the near side, facing front, and hook the reins, the neck piece of the martingale, and the headpiece under the thumb of your left hand. Then push them all forward, clearing my ears. While still holding the headpiece in your left hand, let me *drop* the bit out of my mouth. (It is important to let me open my mouth and free the bit—don't try to pull it out!)

With a twist of the wrist you can slide the bridle over your left forearm, with the browband toward your body, and the martingale and reins in order, ready to be carried to the tack-room. Now both your hands are free to replace my halter on my head. The bridle should be hung up with the browband away from the wall.

Even if you can't completely clean the tack after use, these areas should *always* receive attention:

The girth and the under-side of the saddle should be sponged free of sweat, mud and hair.

The bits should be rinsed off in a bucket of water and wiped clean.

Never put a dirty saddle, girth, or bridle on me. Besides being untidy, the caked dirt will cause sores where it rubs me.

Always turn my head back toward the gate and step through it yourself before turning me loose in the pasture.

If you do this you will never be kicked accidentally if I kick up my heels in delight at being free. (I feel like you do at school recess when I am turned out to pasture—full of play!)

If I am to be taken back to my stall instead of being turned out to pasture, be careful when you lead me through my stall door. Be sure that my body is lined up straight with the opening—and watch as you lead me through to be sure I don't strike a hip on the doorjamb.

After we have entered my stall—don't just unfasten the leadshank and walk out past my hindquarters! If for any reason I should lash out with my heels (I might feel gay at being free again, or I might want to threaten a nosy neighbor who was poking his head over the stall partition) you might be kicked in passing.

Always lead me completely around my stall to the left and back to the doorway. When my head is facing you my heels are a safe distance away, and since you are in a position to step back quickly from my stall and close the door, you cannot possibly be kicked, either by accident or design, while putting me into my stall. Take your time, and be safe!

5. Your Position on Horseback

Earlier I described all the parts of my body, so that you would be able to understand how I move and keep myself in balance. Now we must also make certain that you know exactly where different parts of *your* body are located.

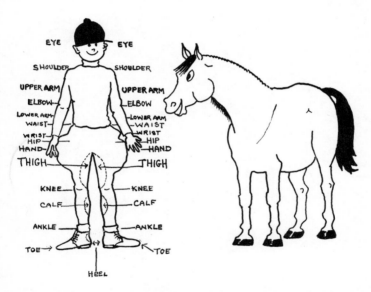

When we start to discuss how you should sit on me and how you should use your body in controlling me, it is very important that you place the *correct* part of your body into the *right* position, and use or move only the proper part when needed.

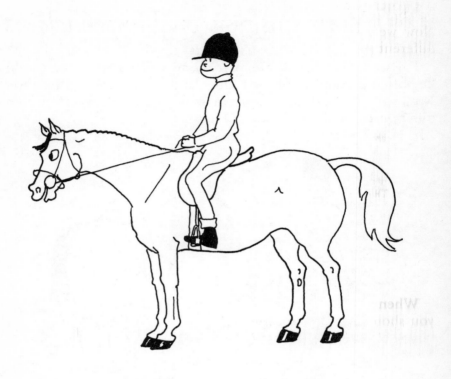

Once you are mounted you will want to get into a position in your saddle which will keep you on my back and which will be the most comfortable for me.

When people first start to ride they often think that the best way to stay on is to hang onto something with their hands (the pommel of the saddle, the reins or a piece of my mane) or to try to wrap their legs around my middle. Believe me, this will not only *not* keep you on—it can prove downright disastrous! You can't stay on my back very long by "hanging on" to any part of me with any part of you.

When you are standing, or walking, or running, you don't hang on to anything to keep from falling—you use the position of your body, changing it as necessary, to keep you in balance. When you ride you will be doing the same thing, using the position of your body to keep you in balance on my back.

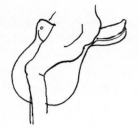

There is only one part of you that will ever "hang on" to anything on me. That will be the muscles of your INNER THIGH, kept close to the saddle at all times, gripping tightly whenever needed to make you secure. This area is called your *seat* in the saddle.

You shouldn't squeeze with your thighs like a nutcracker all the time—they would tire very quickly if you did—but you should always keep them in the proper position, so that they can be tightened quickly whenever necessary.

When first you mount, you should sit in the deepest part of the saddle, with your weight on your THIGHS. Don't sit on a saddle as on a rocking chair, with your shoulders back and your weight on the end of your spine! This puts you completely out of balance and makes me very uncomfortable.

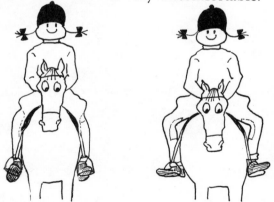

Your KNEE should be close to the saddle flap, pointing toward my shoulder. If your knees are away from my saddle, your thighs will be away, too, and not in the proper position to grip quickly.

Your LOWER LEG should be free at all times, so that you can use it in controlling me.

When not using your leg aid, your foot should be directly under the knee, so that the stirrup leather hangs straight down.

If your lower leg is placed so the foot is ahead of, or behind, the knee, you will find yourself just as much out of balance on my back as you would be if you tried to stand on the ground with both feet a similar distance in front of, or behind, your knee. Try it!

So don't place your leg like this . . .

or this . . .

Your FOOT should be placed in the stirrup with the tread under the ball of your foot, your weight more on the inside than the outside of the foot, and your heel lower than your toe.

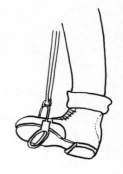

THIGHS

WEIGHT ON INSIDE OF FOOT

THIGHS

WEIGHT ON OUTSIDE OF FOOT

If your weight is on the outside of your foot your thighs will move away from the saddle.

When your heels are up your toes are down; then you are in first diving position, which is the last thing you want to do from my back!

Your ANKLE JOINT can act as a very good shock absorber. If it is kept open it absorbs a great deal of motion that would otherwise bounce you around on my back. Toes far down and heels pulled up locks this spring so that all motion is driven upward where you don't want it.

Your HEAD should be up, with your eyes looking ahead, between my ears.

Your UPPER BODY should be as erect as it would be if you were standing on the ground. However, there should be a *slight hollow in your back,* because your weight will be on your thighs, not on your "tail feathers." Your shoulders should be square and your chest open—not stiff like the statue of a general—but not drooped over like a sack of flour, either!

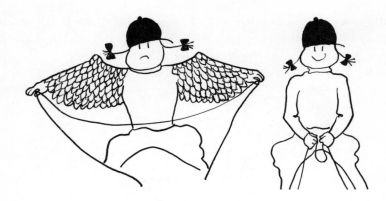

Your UPPER ARM should hang naturally, close to your body. (Don't have your elbows out and flapping like birds' wings.)

Your LOWER ARM and the rein should make a straight line from your elbow to the bit, when viewed from the side.

Your HANDS should be close together, thumb tips facing naturally toward each other; hold the reins in front of the saddle, and low over my withers.

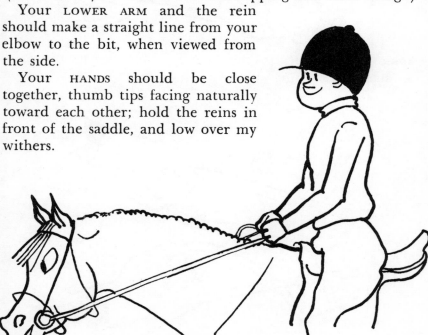

When using only the snaffle rein, you can hold it with all four fingers, the rein entering the hand under the little finger and being kept the right length by squeezing the rein between the thumb and forefinger.

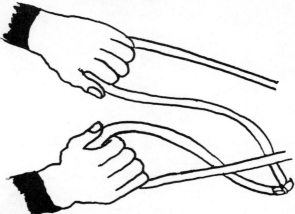

Some people prefer to hold the rein between the little and ring fingers, everything else being the same.

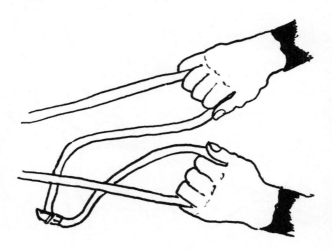

If the bridle has both snaffle and curb reins, the snaffle is held in the same manner as a single rein. The curb then passes between the little and ring fingers, and is also held by the thumb with the snaffle rein.

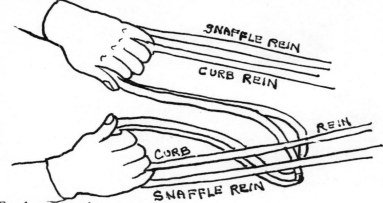

To shorten reins:

To shorten the left rein, open the thumb of your left hand slightly and grasp the end of the left rein between your right thumb and forefinger. Then slip the rein through your left hand to the desired length, and let go of it with your right hand.

To shorten the right rein, reverse this procedure.

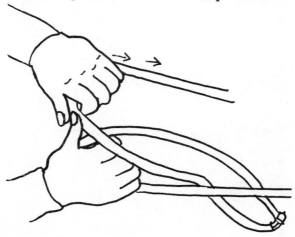

Don't be a **CABBAGE HEAD**!

Don't look down . . .

Look ahead!

Don't be a **WEEPING WILLOW**!

Don't slump over . . .

Sit up straight!

Don't be a **CONCERT PIANIST**!

Don't get your hands above
your elbows . . .

Keep your hands down!

Don't be a flapping **CHICKEN**!

Don't stick out your elbows . . .

Keep your elbows in!

Don't be a BAND LEADER!

Don't separate your hands . . .

Keep your hands close together!

Don't be a GRASSHOPPER!

Don't pull your feet behind you . . .

Keep your feet under your knees!

Don't be a BULLFROG!

Don't have your thighs away from the saddle . . .

Keep your thighs close to the saddle!

Don't be a BALLET DANCER!

Don't turn your toes down . . .

Keep your toes higher than your heels!

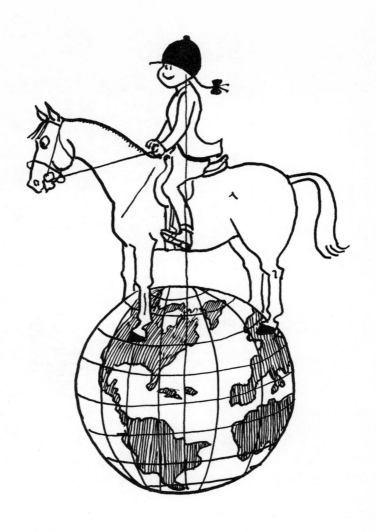

If you are sitting correctly upon my back, your center of gravity will be directly over my center of gravity. You will be in balance with me when you are in this position.

6. Your Controls
and How They Work

Now that you are seated correctly on my back, you will want to know what to do to manage me properly, so I will do what you want me to do, not what I might wish to do at that moment. Your control should and can be easy for you and pleasant for me. I am not your opponent—someone to be overcome by force and punishment, like sparring with a boxer!

Instead, I am like your dancing partner, who will follow your correct guidance willingly.

However, it is very important that your guidance is correct—and that you do not give me mixed signals. Given the correct instructions and assistance, I will be responsive and cooperative and we will be good partners, enjoying each other's company. But if you do not make it clearly understood what you want me to do, or if you make demands in a rough or clumsy way, I will behave exactly as you would under the same conditions. I will do what I intended to do in the first place, and show my annoyance in some way. But it will not be difficult for us to get along together very well, if first you will learn how my body works and how to use the different parts of your body to control mine.

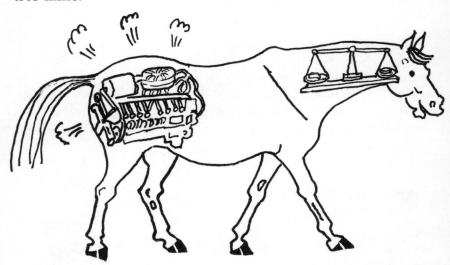

I am made with my "motor" in the rear. All my *impulsion* —which means all my power and push—comes from my hindquarters. I use my forehand to keep my body in balance. By placing my head and neck in different positions, and moving them freely as needed, I can maintain my proper balance.

You could understand this very easily if I could stand on my hind legs and walk beside you. You would discover that your body works in the same manner. You would notice that *your* motor is also located from your hips downward—pushing you along—and that you use the changing position of your upper body to keep in proper balance.

When you are sitting on my back your body from the hips down works with my hindquarters, while your upper body moves with my forehand.

When you first ride me, you must learn how to move with me and how not to interfere with the motions I make to maintain my natural balance. After you become more expert, you will learn how to help me improve my balance, if necessary.

THE AIDS

HANDS

The parts of your body which you use in controlling me are called your *natural aids.*

There are four of these aids. They are:

Your HANDS
Your LEGS
Your WEIGHT
Your VOICE

LEGS

Whenever you ride me, you will always use your hand, leg and weight aids together in some manner, in everything that you ask me to do.

Your voice aid is very helpful at certain times.

BODYWEIGHT

The important thing is to have all your aids giving me the same information at the same time. It is very confusing—and most annoying—to have one of your aids tell me to, "go!" while another aid is saying, "stop!" (In a case like that I simply do whichever I prefer!)

VOICE

90

Your hands control my forehand by means of the reins attached to the bit in my mouth. You use them to guide, check or restrain me, by regulating the impulsion created by my motor in my hindquarters. With them you can alter the height at which I carry my head, and change my balance or my stride.

You should always be in communication with my forehand by the light, feeling contact with my mouth which your hands maintain through the reins at all times.

As soon as you have mounted, shorten your reins until you have this contact with my mouth, holding your hands together, in front of the saddle and low over my withers.

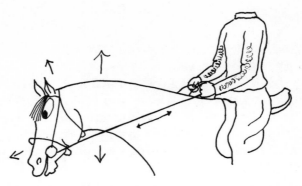

When I am moving, you should keep your arms relaxed, so that your hands can follow the balancing motions of my head and neck. In this way you can always maintain a continuing, light contact but will not interfere with the use of my forehand to maintain my balance.

If you did not give and take with my balancing motions, I would feel just as you would if your arms were tied to your sides, so that you could not properly keep yourself in balance.

It would be possible for you to walk or run, but it would be awkward, difficult and uncomfortable. The discomfort would annoy you very much, and you would soon make an effort to free yourself.

If my balancing motions are hampered, I, too, try to free myself. I may toss my head or push it toward the ground, in an effort to loosen the reins. If I am too uncomfortable, I may stop and refuse to go. Can you blame me?

To use the bit for control, you increase the light contact which you have with my mouth until there is pressure on either or both sides of my jaw. This contact should be increased and strengthened only as much as is necessary for me to respond. I will respond agreeably to light, repeated, increasing pressures —while I will forcibly resist a strong, steady pull on my jaw!

The pressure can be increased by tightening your fingers on the reins, turning your wrists or slightly stiffening your forearms.

Never brace yourself and pull against my jaw!
A steady, unyielding pull on my jaw is very painful to me. Continuous pulling makes the bars of my jaw numb and insensitive, so I cannot respond properly to the bit.

If you pull me, I will pull right back.
This is a tug-of-war which I can easily win!
The yielding motions of your hands should be toward the bit, the restraining ones toward your body.

Never raise or separate your hands in order to increase pressure on my jaw.

If you find it necessary to put your hands in either of these positions, your reins have become too long and should be shortened to their proper length.

Don't ride with your reins taut—
remember, it interferes with my balance and hurts and numbs my jaw!

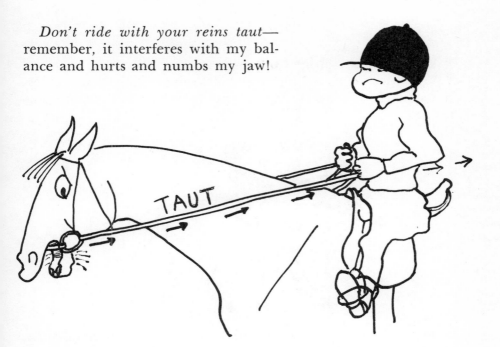

Just try to imagine how you would feel if you had a metal bit in your mouth! Then you will realize how important it is to have a light contact with my mouth, with the reins held in sensitive, feeling hands.

Don't ride with your reins slack—
then you and I are out of communication.

Do ride with contact!

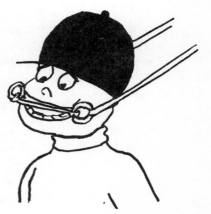

Your legs control my hindquarters.

You use them by placing your calves against my sides, immediately behind the girth, and squeezing and tapping, as needed.

Your two legs are used together to make and maintain the energy and impulsion of the "motor" in my hindquarters. Your legs can also be used to diminish energy and impulsion.

Your legs are used separately to push, or restrain, my hindquarters in any direction.

The amount of pressure needed for this control depends on many things. Horses vary just as humans do in their reactions and temperaments. Some are lazy or slow or stolid—or just plain stubborn. They will need strong and continuous use of your legs to start and keep their "motors" running. Other horses are active, quick, alert and responsive. They will need only the slightest and most tactful use of your legs to control their hindquarters. And, of course, there will be all degrees and shades of response between these extremes. Always start with the least possible pressure, and add to it as you find it necessary.

To touch my sides at the correct place with the proper part of your leg, you must make use of the "rotary" joint in your knee. This rotary joint enables you to turn your foot outward slightly, so that when your leg is drawn back the pressure will be directed against my side, instead of swinging your leg past it.

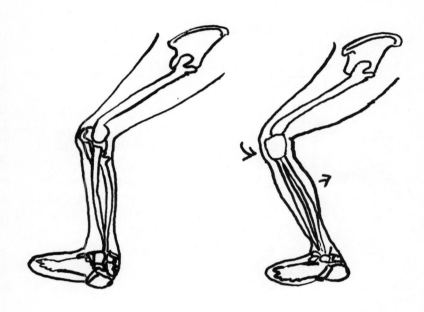

The calf of your leg should be against my side *before* you apply pressure. I will respond agreeably to the repeated, rhythmic squeezings of your calf muscles. Sometimes I may need a little more encouragement, and then your legs may be moved a bit away from my sides and applied with a more vigorous, tapping motion.

But never, never should your leg be swung like a baseball bat, striking my side with a big thump!

I would feel just as you would if someone suddenly struck you a blow between your shoulders! Both of us would be sent forward by the force of such unpleasant blows—but the motion gained this way would be uneven, unsustained and uncontrolled— and very much resisted and resented.

However, I will move just as willingly from the squeezing or tapping of your legs as you would from the steady, repeated pressures of a firm hand placed behind your shoulder.

Don't jab me in the side with the point of your heel!

I like that just as much as you do a good poke in the ribs—not at all!

Don't let your legs hang like spaghetti —use them!

Remember, in order to keep my motor going after it is started, you must continue to use your leg aid.

WEIGHT AID

Your weight aid helps you to control my rate of speed and to keep me in balance.

In using your body weight to maintain your own balance on my back, your upper body moves forward from the hips, according to the increase of my speed (or the increase you are asking me to make) just as it would keep you in balance if you were walking or running at this same rate of speed.

100

Your forward shift of weight makes it easier for me to go faster, by lightening the load on my motor (hindquarters); I connect this movement of your body with an increase in speed, so I get ready to go faster.

In slowing down, your upper body comes back toward its original erect position, just as it would if you were decreasing your speed on the ground. The return of weight to my motor area has a braking action; I remember that this change of body position is connected with decreasing speed, so I prepare to slow down.

In my circles and turns, your weight aid helps to keep me in balance. With your hips square with my hips and your shoulders square with my shoulders, your weight will be on your inside seat bone, with the heel on that side well down.

Used with your leg aid, the pressure of your body weight upon your seat bones helps to send me forward.

Having your upper body too far forward for the rate of speed I am going puts you out of balance and also overloads my forehand, making me inclined to stumble.

Holding your upper body too far back is another wrong position; it unbalances you and slows me down by burdening my motor.

Your voice is a very useful aid in communicating with me. The tone of your voice is important in its use.

The word "whoa" means "stop" to me. If you want me to stop completely, use your voice with a tone of command. (If you just want me to go a little more slowly, use your voice soothingly.)

A calm voice will help to quiet me when I am excited or frightened.

A clucking noise of your tongue can make me increase speed, but *don't* use your voice this way to make me go faster. Riding all by yourself you may become lazy and forget how to use your leg aids, by depending on your voice alone to do the job for you.

When riding in company it is very inconsiderate to use your voice aid for increase of speed. *Your* voice can be heard by your companion's pony and he may think this encouragement was meant for him, creating problems of control for his rider.

Fear in your voice frightens me! Never scream or shout when you are riding me.

105

Now that you have learned about your four aids and how to use them, you will be able to let me know exactly what you want me to do. This understanding will make it possible for you and me to enjoy a very successful friendship.

106

7. How to Start, Stop and Steer

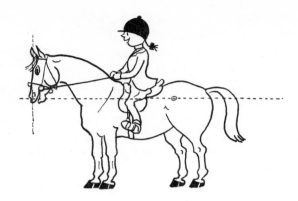

Before starting my motor and putting me into motion, be sure that you are in the correct position in the saddle—looking ahead between my ears!

Contact with my mouth should start when my neck is stretched forward comfortably, since I balance myself at my ordinary walk with a lengthened neck. However, this does not mean that my head should be allowed to hang down, with my nose below my chest. In this position there will be too much weight on my forehand. (If you were to walk with your neck thrust forward and your head hanging down, you would be out of balance, too.) My nose should be on about an even line with my hips to be in the best balance and control, and my head, seen from the side, should be almost straight up and down, with my nose a little out in front.

To raise my head, squeeze with your legs as if to send me forward, but resist this forward movement with your hands. This will bring my head up into a proper position and help me to accept the bit's action in my mouth.

107

Make sure that this contact has been made with your reins an even length. Otherwise my head may be carried a bit to one side. If you can see the eye on one side of my head more easily than the other, you will know that the rein on that side is shorter, turning my head in that direction. Make the necessary change in your reins to assure even contact before we move off.

It is most important that my body is kept in a *straight line* from my head to my tail, in order for me to move properly. If my head and neck are swinging to one side or the other, or my hindquarters are out of line with the rest of my body, I will move just as awkwardly as you would if you walked or ran with your body twisted.

You will be using your hands to keep my head and neck in line in front of my shoulders, and your legs to keep my hindquarters straight behind my shoulders.

Your leg aids will start my motor when we are ready to go, beginning with gentle, even squeezes of your calves behind my girth, increasing this pressure until I start forward.

Your arms should relax, letting your hands move forward while keeping continuous light contact as I stretch my neck to step forward.

Your upper body will incline forward as much as it would if you were about to walk on the ground. This change in position will be very slight, but it will keep you in balance and also will serve as a weight aid in helping to get me to move. You should drive your seat bones well down in the saddle to assist in moving me forward.

Use your voice aid ("clucking") only if necessary and only if you can do it quietly, for your pony's ears alone.

4-beat gait

THE WALK

When you put me into motion, start out at the first and slowest gait, the walk. My walk is a "four-beat" gait, for each of my four feet hits the ground separately. The first step is taken by one of my hind legs (driven by my "motor") pushing my forehand forward. The next step will be made by the diagonally opposite foreleg. The third step will be another pushing stride from the other hind leg. And the fourth step is taken by the remaining opposite foreleg.

WALK

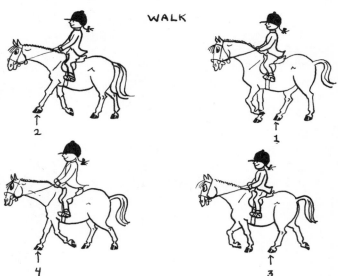

The footprint made by my hindleg at the walk will fall at or a little beyond the footprint of the foreleg on the same side.

The rising and falling movements of my shoulders and hips, as I take my walking steps, and the action created by my driving hindquarters make motions which affect your seat.

You do not want this slight motion (like a boat rocking on a gentle swell) to disturb your seat. It should not cause your upper leg to slide back and forth in the saddle, or upset your balance by making your lower leg swing forward and backward. You must let your upper body absorb this motion, and move easily with my movements. Don't stiffen the muscles in your upper body, or your seat will slide and your lower leg will swing!

My head and neck must move, too, keeping me in balance. Let your hands follow those balancing motions.

The alternate, squeezing pressures of your legs, applied first to one side of my body and then to the other, set and maintain the rate of speed at which I will walk. This pressure should be applied on the side of the hind leg which is about to leave the ground in order to be effective.

I will go in the direction in which my head is pointed. But when you want to change the direction in which I am going—remember that I have two ends to turn. . . .

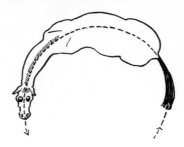

While your hands guide the forehand in the desired direction, your legs and body weight should keep the hindquarters following in the line of the curve behind the forehand.

The way my body is made my legs can move forward and backward only—they cannot move out to the side as yours can. So I have to be moved forward before I can turn. If you try to drag me around by pulling my head you may make me step on myself and cause a painful injury.

So don't make the mistake of trying to turn me from a standstill! *Put me into forward motion first!*

112

Your turning hand brings the rein back toward your body center, directing my head, while your opposite hand moves forward an equal amount, to lengthen the rein on that side so my head and neck are free to turn.

Your leg on the turning side (known as your "inside leg") pushes my hindquarters in the opposite direction, to keep them following after my forehand. Your "outside leg" (the leg away from the turning side) is used as needed to keep me going at the same steady pace. I need constant impulsion from my motor to turn easily. If my motor slows down during the turning process, I become difficult for you to manage and my turn will be awkward. Keep squeezing with the outside leg to keep me moving steadily.

RIGHT TURN

LEFT TURN

In turns, your weight aid helps to keep me in balance. With your hips square with my hips and your shoulders square with my shoulders, your weight will be on your seat bones in the direction of the turn, with the inside heel well down.

113

Next, you must know how to slow down and to stop my motor.

First, steady your seat in the saddle, to be secure for a change of speed. Then bring your upper body back to the position that will be in balance at the lower rate of speed wanted (or to its original erect position, if I am to come to a full halt). This change will not only keep you in balance but will also make use of your weight aid to help decrease my forward motion.

With your seat bones pressed well down in the saddle, close your legs firmly against my sides next to the girth, while your hands prevent my forward movement, alternately tightening and easing the pressure on the reins. *Be sure* to relax any tension on my mouth as soon as I have stopped.

Before adding any pressure on my jaw, use your voice aid to let me know that you want me to slow down or stop. The "whoa" that I associate with decrease of speed helps prepare me to cooperate with your other aids for slowing down—and sometime, if you drop a rein or lose a stirrup iron, my attention to a firm "whoa" can save the situation from getting out of hand!

While you are not permitted to use the voice aid to decrease speed in some riding competitions (such as dressage tests) it may be used properly and safely under most other conditions.

When riding in company, it is perfectly all right for you to say "whoa" to your pony. It won't cause any problems for your companion even if his pony, on hearing your voice command, slows down, too. (There is no danger involved in slowing down, while danger can be involved in going faster.)

Start using your restraining aids well ahead of the point at which you wish me to stop. Remember that it takes a moment for me to get these messages from you and another moment for me to start putting them into action. If I am going fast it will take a certain time and distance for my "motor" to be slowed down and stopped. So don't try to jam on the brakes at the last minute—it won't work!

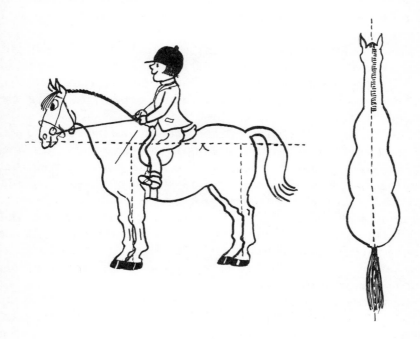

After I have stopped, I should stand squarely upon my four legs, with my body straight—and you should sit correctly on my back, not slumped over in a heap.

When you first practice your proper position on my back and the correct use of your aids, it is best to ride in a small area that is enclosed by a fence or wall, such as a riding ring or paddock. Until your seat is secure and you are sufficiently familiar with your aids to be able to count on your ability to use them effectively, do not take me out in open fields or on roads and trails. Don't ride, either, along with others who are unaware of your limited experience, or who are unwilling to ride in the places and at the speed which is safe for you as a beginner.

You should not put me in any situation in which I might become excited or frightened, or in which I might want to increase speed for some reason. This would frighten you, too, and you probably could not act calmly enough to bring me under control.

Just being in the wide open spaces themselves gives me a sense of freedom that often tempts me to stretch my legs and have a good gallop. I quickly realize in an enclosed area that there is no place to go but around and around, so I am not inspired to hurry. After one or two trips around, I will become familiar with all that is to be seen in a ring, and will not suddenly come upon strange sights or sounds to startle me, as might happen on a cross-country ride where there are scampering rabbits and barking dogs, or on the road, with speeding, horn-blowing automobiles.

In a ring or paddock, the ground will be level, or nearly so. Thus you will avoid the additional problems of changing position and using stronger aids that become necessary when going up and down hills, and you won't be distracted by having to watch out for ditches, holes, rocks or rough going as you would be while riding over hilly ground cross-country.

By riding on a track fairly close to the fence or wall, you have something else that helps keep me straight, and this also makes your task easier.

116

If others are riding with you in this place, be sure to keep a safe distance (at least two horse's lengths) behind the rider in front of you. If your pony overtakes this rider, do not pass close by! His pony might kick at yours in passing, and you or your pony might be needlessly hurt.

Do not stop on the track, for this will make problems for the rider coming behind you, and also make it necessary for you to start my motor again.

If no one is riding behind you, you may turn off the track and make a circle, returning to the track at the spot where you left it. This will give the pony ahead of you time to move a safe distance away from you. Otherwise, you should cross the ring to an unoccupied space that is not too close to another pony.

If you wish to move closer to the fence, while continuing around the ring, use your hand aid on the side of the fence to guide my forehand in that direction and the leg aid on the opposite side to push my hindquarters over into line with my forehand.

117

Just as the choice of where you ride me makes a difference in your ease of control, your choice of what you wear while riding also can help or hinder the security of your seat and your ability to use your aids properly.

Riding breeches are made especially for this purpose. They are made of materials (usually woolen) that adhere to the leather of the saddle, making it easier to have a tight seat when necessary. They are cut in a special pattern that permits plenty of room for bending the hips and knees, but prevents the cloth from turning or bunching up on the leg.

Jodphur breeches, which go all the way down to the ankle, and which are worn with a short *jodphur boot,* are the most practical breeches for most riding use, especially for beginners and young, still-growing riders. The cloth over the calf permits a delicate feeling between the rider's leg and the pony's side which is hard to obtain in a high leather boot unless the boot fits perfectly, having been made to your particular measure out of fine soft skins. (Such a boot is naturally quite costly, and it would be foolish to purchase a new pair every six months or so as your feet grow larger and your legs longer.)

Jodphur boots provide the necessary solid sole and deep heel for proper placement and support on the stirrup iron, and have enough height to protect the ankle from any chafing by the top of the iron. These come ready-made in inexpensive styles, so there is no great loss when they are outgrown and must be replaced. The cheaper high boots are made out of the coarse parts of the cowhide. They make a stiff, unyielding shell around the lower leg that prevents all feeling between rider and pony. This is the last thing you want to have happen!

So don't buy cheap high boots—they will hinder, not help your riding.

Whenever you are mounted, wear protective headgear. A well-fitting *hunting cap* will protect your head from injury in case of a fall. *This is a MUST when you ride!*

Any loose, comfortable jacket will serve for general riding. If you progress to riding in competition or going foxhunting, you will want a proper *riding coat,* which is made of lightweight material for summer use and tweed or heavy melton cloth for cold-weather protection when hunting.

A polo shirt is suitable for warm-weather wear, a turtleneck sweater for cooler days or to be worn under coat or jacket. A shirt with four-in-hand tie is proper to wear under a regular riding coat, a white stock is worn with a melton hunting coat.

Though you may have to start your riding in blue jeans or slacks, you should buy an inexpensive pair of jodphurs as soon as possible. When you begin to ride a bit faster, you will find that loose trousers of slippery material makes it difficult for you to keep a secure seat. Blue jeans or Levis are best suited to riding in a Western stock saddle.

If you must start your riding without jodphur boots, wear some sort of sturdy, tie-on shoe with a solid sole. The familiar "loafer" moccasin-type shoe is not suitable, because in your efforts to keep the shoe from dropping off your heel you will force your toes down—where they don't belong! "Sneakers" are even worse, for they give no support in the sole and, having no heel, can permit your foot to slip all the way through the iron if it is a bit too big.

8. How to Trot, and Back Up

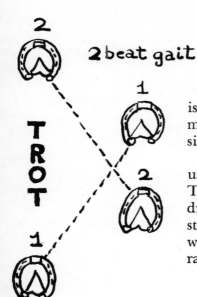

2 beat gait

My next faster gait is the TROT. This is a "two-beat" gait in which one of my hindlegs and the diagonally opposite foreleg move together.

I can move faster at the trot by using my legs in this combination. The push from my hindquarters that drives me forward at the trot is much stronger than the one I use when I walk, and my legs move much more rapidly.

When you first experience the motion of the trot you will find that it is somewhat unsettling (or perhaps even unseating) if you do not first learn what to do to stay in balance and be secure on my back when I trot.

The slow, easy motion of my walk, which resembles the motion of a boat at anchor rocking on a gently rolling swell, suddenly changes to a series of rapid, tilting, jolting bounces. Your boat has gotten into rough surf, and is being rocked from side to side, shot forward and then dropped into the trough between the breakers, before being shot forward on the next wave. Be careful that you don't capsize!

To balance myself in my trotting gait, I change the position in which I carried my head and neck at the walk, by raising my head and shortening my neck somewhat. If you notice me when I am completely free at pasture you will see that this is my natural manner of balancing myself.

This change of head and neck position will make the length of rein which was correct for contact at the walk too long when I start to trot. So when you are preparing to change my gait from the walk to the trot, you must first shorten your reins an inch or so. Be sure to make the change in your reins before starting to trot, and do it as quietly as possible.

To change gait from the walk to the trot, you have to speed up my motor by using your leg aids, both legs squeezing at the same time, with increasing pressures, until I move off into my trot.

As always, your hands should maintain a light, even contact. As I need much less balancing motion of my head and neck at the trot than I did at the walk, your hands should remain quite steady, with very little motion. (Don't let the motion of the trot send them pumping up and down! Keep them low over my withers, where they belong.)

Your body weight will be inclined forward according to the speed at which I am trotting, just as it would be inclined if you were running at the same rate of speed on the ground.

By the time you have started to ride at the trot, I hope that you will have practiced using your legs, hands, and weight aids together so well that you won't need to call on your voice aid to help start or keep my motor running!

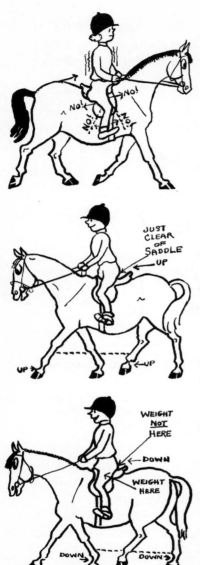

Be sure to tighten your seat in the saddle before changing to this more active gait.

When you first start me to trot, you will sit to the motion, just as you sat to my walking motion. This is called a *sitting trot*. But it won't be as easy—because there is going to be a lot more and a different motion! So don't let those lower legs swing or upper legs slide; keep your legs steady, with feet under knees and thighs close to saddle while you absorb this new movement in your upper body.

After I have taken a few trotting strides, you will begin to allow your upper body to be moved by the force of only one of these driving hindlegs. This force will send your upper body slightly more forward and upward, just enough to clear the saddle. While your upper body is thus clear of the saddle, it escapes the thrust of the other hindleg. As your upper body returns to its original position, it again receives the drive of the hindleg with which it first moved.

You must be careful to hold your weight properly on your *thighs* when you return to the saddle, and not plop down on the end of your spine!

126

This rhythmic rise and fall of your body in time with the driving force of one hindleg at the trot is known as *posting* to the trot.

At the trot, as at all other times, you need to stay as deep in and close to your saddle as possible, in order to be in the best balance and most secure position on my back.

The thrust your body receives from the hindquarters of ponies or horses which you may ride will vary greatly in strength and rapidity, depending upon the particular individual's "motor" power and *conformation* (which means how his entire structure is made). Some horses move you very little from your saddle at the trot, while others send you quite high into the air, if you do not make the right effort to direct and limit this drive.

Controlling this drive is done by tightening your thighs to prevent too much forward thrust, and by tucking your seat bones under so the motion becomes one of rolling slightly *forward and under,* rather than that of your "tail feathers" shooting up and down behind you! If you find yourself rising high out of the saddle each time my hind legs throw you up, you can be sure you're not tucking in your tail feathers!

127

The correct position of your foot in the stirrup iron (with the "shock absorber" in your ankle well open) helps you absorb some of the jolting I create when I trot. Some of this motion can be passed from your upper body to your ankle joint, by allowing this "shock absorber" to receive some of the force; as your upper body rises in posting, your heel is driven slightly lower. This second means of absorbing and disposing of the motion created by my hindquarters in my trotting stride is very helpful in keeping you close to your saddle.

Remember, posting is a way of moving with my motion at the trot, in a manner which keeps you secure and in perfect balance. When you post in rhythmic harmony with me, you will be able to ride me at the trot easily and comfortably.

Unfortunately, many riders at the beginning see the up and down motion of posting to the trot and think that this movement is one which they should create, pushing themselves up and down in the saddle by bracing their feet against the stirrup irons like so many bullfrogs about to leap off a lily pad! This bad habit works very much against the security of their seat and makes it difficult for them to control their ponies at that gait. Don't *you* make this error!

The "pushing off the irons and up into the air" movement moves you up and out of your secure seat position. It also flings your upper body too far forward for correct balance, if your feet are braced in the irons behind your knees; and if your feet are braced in front of your knees, it makes your body topple backwards and unbalances you completely.

If you push yourself up and down when I am trotting, you will have difficulty in moving in time with me, besides wasting a lot of your energy needlessly!

So don't make the very bad mistake of using your stirrup irons as your base of support, standing on them with your ankle joints closed.

Since my legs move in diagonally opposite combinations at the trot, if you are out of the saddle when my right hindleg leaves the ground, you will also be out of the saddle when my left foreleg is off the ground; you will return to the saddle as my right hind and left foreleg return to the ground.

When you rise from and return to the saddle in time with the rise and fall of my left foreleg, you are said to be *posting on the left diagonal*. If you are moving with my right foreleg, you are said to be *posting on the right diagonal*.

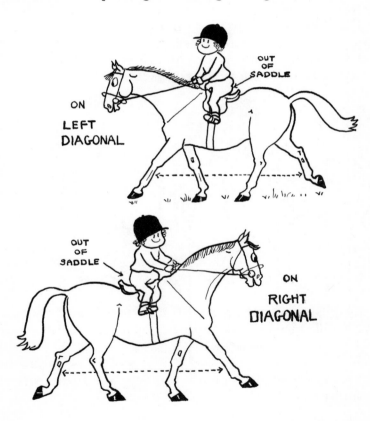

To be able to tell on which diagonal you are posting, watch one of my shoulder blades as it moves forward and backward. If you are out of the saddle as it moves forward and return as it comes back, you will be posting on that diagonal. If you wish to change diagonals, sit to one extra stride of my trot and then let yourself rise into a posting trot at the next stride.

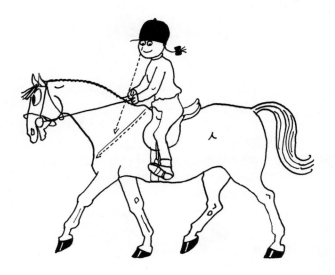

When making a circle or turning to change direction, you should always post with the diagonal on the outside of the circle. This will let me use my inside hind leg to push you into your posting. It is easier for me to carry your weight on a circle if you post on the correct diagonal.

In riding in any ordinary situation (down roads and trails or cross-country) it is a good idea to change occasionally the diagonal on which you are posting, in order to let me use my back muscles evenly.

To use your leg aid to set, maintain or increase my rate of speed at the trot, squeeze with both legs at the same time, as you return to the saddle in your post, to make me reach forward into my next stride.

When you are ready to change from the trot back to the walk, first you should change from posting to sitting to my trot.

132

With tightened seat, and legs held firmly at my girth, you should return your body weight to the position for balance at the walk.

Remember to use your voice aid for decrease of speed, before applying and releasing pressures to my jaw with your hands.

As I come back to a walk, slightly lengthen the reins again as I stretch my neck, in order to resume the correct contact for that gait.

You will find that learning to post is rather like learning to ice-skate or to ride a bicycle. At first it may seem quite difficult but you can learn it quite quickly if you persist. Then you will be able to post ever afterward, without giving much thought to it.

BACKING

In order for me to step backward easily, I must first stand straight and squarely on all four legs.

I step backward in the same diagonal sequence of steps I use for the trot. My left hindleg pushes me backward and the right foreleg steps at the same time. Then my right hindleg pushes back for the next stride, and my left foreleg steps in unison.

To get me to back, you must first sit in the proper position for putting me into motion. What you do then is to put me into motion with your legs and weight aids but before I can step forward, you resist this forward motion by increasing the tension on the reins and directing the motion backward instead. In otherwords, your legs apply equal pressure to create impulsion in my "motor" while your hands direct this energy backward.

I should always go backward in a straight line. If my hind-quarters swing to the right you use your right leg, drawn back from the girth, to press it back into line; if it swings to the left, your left leg must straighten me.

I should move backward in distinct strides, and not drag my legs. *Never* try to *pull* me backward, on my jaw!

When you first practice backing, it is best to try only one or two steps.

I should halt squarely, ready to step forward easily.

9. How to Canter, Gallop, and Jump

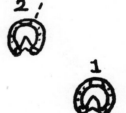

CANTER

3

2

2

1

3-beat gait

I have a third natural gait, called the CANTER. This is a "three-beat" gait, in which I move my legs in this order:

I push off with one hindleg; the foreleg on the same side and the opposite hindleg take the next stride together; and finally the opposite foreleg takes the third stride.

Then I push off again with the hindleg that took the first step and continue with the same sequence of footfalls.

For example . . .

(1) Left hindleg, alone, pushes me forward; (2) Right hindleg and left foreleg together carry weight forward until...(3) Right foreleg takes over and lifts me into the air, to come down again on (1) Left hindleg, etc.

In this gait, the foreleg which strikes alone (3) is known as the "leading foreleg," and I am said to be on the *right* or *left lead*, according to which foreleg is leading.

If I am moving on a circle, I should lead with the foreleg on the inside of the circle in order to balance myself most easily.

By nature, I do not carry myself straight at the canter. I move somewhat sideways, as you would if you were skipping. The shoulder and hip on the side of the leading foreleg will be slightly in advance of the opposite shoulder and hip. My head will be turned just a little in the direction of my lead, and my hindquarters will be carried markedly in that direction.

This way of moving sends me forward in a series of bounding strides, a motion with which you can easily learn to stay in balance. The canter should be very comfortable for you to ride and give you a most enjoyable sensation, due to the very rhythmic swing of the gait.

It is *possible* for me to change quite easily from a trot into a canter—you often see me do it when I am free in pasture . . .

. . . but the results are not always successful when you try to get me to canter by making me trot faster—and faster—and faster!

When you are riding me, you will want complete control over the point at which I start to canter, over the lead on which I canter on and the rate of speed at which I start.

To have this control, you should start my canter either from the halt (which means I am standing still) or the walk, rather than the trot.

The chances are very slim that I would start cantering at the *exact place* you wanted me to begin, there would be no guarantee as to which lead I would use. Also, by being made to trot so fast that I more or less stumble into my canter, I would be quite out of balance (and so would you!) with much too much weight on my forehand. So all in all, it is a crude and unsatisfactory way to start a canter.

When you are just beginning to learn how to canter, you may find it necessary to let me trot into my canter, but the sooner you learn how to start my canter from the halt or the walk, the sooner you will have complete control of when, where and how I canter.

In order for me to spring with the greatest of ease into my cantering stride, I should first be somewhat *"collected."* When I am collected I am able to use my body with the least effort, because my motor is charged with energy and my jaw is relaxed, responding willingly to your hands.

You may have often seen me naturally collected when I have been free in pasture. My hindquarters seem to be filled with extra power; they are slightly lowered and my hindlegs reach well under my body, taking more of its weight than usual. My head is raised and my neck slightly arched and my forelegs seem to scarcely touch the ground, my forehand has become so light. From this collected state I can go into any gait with ease and rapidity.

When I am collected, my hindquarters have more power and my forehand has more freedom of movement. My entire body is slightly shortened, like a coiled spring. And when that spring uncoils—I can bound forward with the greatest of ease!

In order for you to collect me, your legs will need to apply the necessary pressures to fill my motor with energy while your hands restrain this energy from escaping until the moment for my canter. This driving force, kept under control, tends to bring my hocks farther forward beneath my body, lowering my hindquarters slightly. As more of my weight moves back toward my hindquarters, my forehand lightens and my head and neck are raised, with my jaw relaxing, or *flexing*, at the *poll*, to the light pressure of your rein. (My lower jaw is hinged at the poll, behind my ears. When the muscles where it is hinged relax, my jaw gives to the pressure of your hands. This is known as flexing.)

When you have filled my motor with energy by the use of your legs, pressing vigorously behind the girth, and I feel to you as if I *want* to go forward at a faster gait even though your hands prevent me from breaking into a trot, then this forward-driving force will raise my head and neck until my forehand feels quite light in your hands—and you will know that I should be able to make a correct *strike-off* without effort.

145

The point at which I change my gait into the canter is known as my strike-off into the canter. When you are ready to have me canter, these are the preparations which you will make for my strike-off.

First—you should tighten your seat in the saddle, as you always should before every change of gait, pace or direction!

When I canter, my head will be raised somewhat and my neck will shorten from the balancing position it had for the walk. Thus, in order to maintain proper contact, you will have to adjust the rein length again before I start to canter.

This elevation of my head and neck comes from the driving force of my hindquarters—created by the pressures of your leg aids.

Don't try to pull my head up with your hands!

146

Your body position should not change until after I have begun my cantering strides. In my strike-off, my forehand should be as free of weight as possible, as it has to be lifted into the first springing stride of the canter. If your upper body weight hangs forward over one of my shoulders (as you may see many riders mistakenly doing!) it burdens my forehand and makes it more difficult for me to do an easy strike-off. Keep your upper body erect in the saddle until I have begun to canter.

Your hands and legs must always work together to get me ready for my strike-off into the canter.

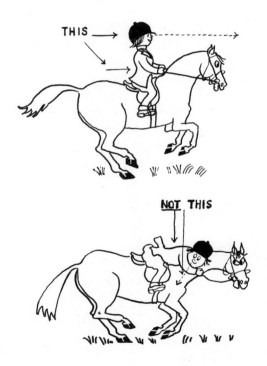

AIDS
FOR
CANTER
(RIGHT LEAD)

RIGHT
SIDE
VIEW

If I am to take my right lead, your right leg must remain opposite the girth while your left leg is drawn back to press my hindquarters to the right. This places my body weight over my right hindleg, and frees my left hindleg so that it can push off on the right lead. With your right hand you should flex my head slightly to the right, and then relax tension on the reins enough to release my pent-up energy; I will spring forward into my cantering stride.

LEFT
SIDE
VIEW

AIDS
FOR
CANTER
(RIGHT LEAD)

When you first practice the use of
your aids for the strike-off into the
canter, ride in a circle in the direction
of the lead which you wish to take.

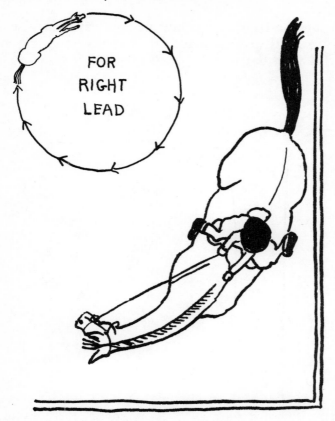

FOR
RIGHT
LEAD

It is very helpful, whenever possible, to start the canter as I
am rounding the corner of the *manège,* which is the name for a
riding ring. My body at that moment is in a good position to
strike-off into a canter.

You will find the canter an easy and comfortable gait to ride. You will sit to it much as you sat to the walk, your thighs and lower legs staying in position and your upper body taking the motion created by this stride, with your seat bones staying close to the saddle.

You do not rise from the saddle in any way that resembles posting to the trot! (You will see other riders bouncing at the canter in this way, but it is a very bad error!)

As I spring forward into a cantering stride, the sensation is much like swinging in a swing. Just as you arch your back and push to send a swing aloft, so you swing forward with each of my strides. This keeps you in balance and helps to send me forward into my next stride.

Your legs should be used together to apply pressures to set, maintain or increase the rate of speed at which I canter. This pressure should be applied just as the leading foreleg strikes the ground, in order to act upon the hindleg which is just about to push off into the next stride. (This timing will take practice, too!)

Your hands should move with the balancing motions of my head and neck in the swinging movement of this gait.

Your weight must move forward in accordance with the rate of speed at which I canter; this can be as slow as a slow trot, a very rapid pace, or any of the degrees between.

To slow down at the canter or to return to the trot or walk, your aids are used the same way they were used to decrease speed at the other gaits:

Close your legs, opposite the girth; return your body weight to the position of balance for the new gait; use your voice firmly, and restrain with hands, using alternate checking and releasing pressures.

When you first learned to use your aids to get me to move and start to walk it seemed very difficult to get the different parts of your body to do the right things at the right time. By practicing starting, stopping and turning, and setting and changing the rate of speed at which I walked, soon you gained confidence in the fact that the aids, used together properly, really do work to control me. Since the aids that change a walk to a trot are very much like those used to start the walk, it is not hard to learn how to change gait from the walk to the trot.

Starting to canter is a much more difficult task, however, because the use of the aids has to be very *exact*, and *timing* is of great importance. So, don't be discouraged if you don't succeed immediately. If you thought that I was properly prepared to canter and I just raced off into a fast trot, check to see what may have gone wrong.

It's like baking bread; all the ingredients have to go into the batter in the right amounts before the dough will rise. In the same way, if you want to have a successful strike-off, all the right ingredients have to go into it, not only in the right amounts but also at the right moments!

RECIPE FOR A SUCCESSFUL CANTER STRIKE-OFF

No matter how much energy I have in my motor, I won't canter if you let it escape through your hands and permit me to trot instead; or if you let my head and neck hang down, weighing down my forehand; or if you don't put me in position to strike off into a cantering stride.

There can still be no success, even with my head and neck raised and my body in the correct position, if there is not enough *energy* to send my body springing forward.

NO ENERGY!

DEAD MOTOR!

It will take effort, practice and patience to learn how to get me properly collected, with my motor running at just the right speed and my position correct, before you release my energy for the strike-off. It will take repeated attempts to get the feeling and the timing for this correct beginning for the canter. But you will be very well rewarded indeed when you are able to start me off properly, at the place of your choice, on the lead you elect, and in the position from which we can start to canter together with the greatest of ease and in perfect balance with each other.

I am made in such a way that I cannot stride beyond the tip of my nose. If my head is raised and my neck shortened (as they are when I am collected) my strides will be shortened accordingly. If I have a great deal of impulsion from my hindquarters, but my head and neck are raised so that I cannot go into a longer stride, then my knees and hocks will rise as well as go forward. This is spoken of as knee and hock *action*.

The more my head and neck extend at the canter the greater the length of my stride.

My fastest gait is the gallop, which is an extension of my cantering stride. My legs move in the same sequence, but because of the greater forward drive from my hindquarters there is a moment of suspension when all four of my feet are off the ground. Since I want to cover as much ground as possible at the gallop, my head and neck stretch to their full length, permitting the greatest possible length of my stride. My forelegs reach out well in front of me, and my driving hindlegs swing far forward under my body.

When I move at the gallop, your weight should move well forward and a strong contact should be kept with my mouth. However, since I am more difficult to control at the gallop (with my head and nose thrust forward) and you won't have much reason to go *that* fast, unless you are competing in a race, I strongly advise you to stick to the canter!

By the time you can canter well, there will be a lot of reasons why you will want to learn how to ride me over obstacles or to *jump,* as it is called.

In riding cross-country on woodland trails we may encounter fallen logs which are awkward to get around. If you have a chance to go foxhunting, we will need to jump fences in order to follow the hounds. In Pony Club Rally competitions, there are obstacles to jump in the Cross-Country and Stadium Jumping phases. And—if we become quite expert—we may want to enter a jumping class at a Horse Show!

So you'll want to learn how to be secure on my back when I jump an obstacle and also how to help me instead of interfering with me while I'm doing it.

In discussing jumping, we can divide the process into four parts: the Approach, the Take-Off, the Flight and the Landing.

The APPROACH is our preparation. The distance from which we start is determined by the height and width of the obstacle and kind of jump I have to make. Until you have had enough experience to decide the best distance for an approach, use at least ten times my length. It is important for you to head me directly for the center of the obstacle, with my body straight from head to tail. (My body is said to be *in alignment* when it is lined up correctly.) It is also important that you look straight ahead between my ears, sighting the center of the obstacle.

Actually, jumping over an obstacle is much like a higher and longer spring in my cantering stride. And all the rules which you learned for cantering apply to riding me over an obstacle. Your seat must be tightened and the reins shortened; I should be collected, with the energy you create in my motor contained in your hands; my head and neck should be raised and my forehand lightened, just as if you were preparing to canter.

I do not need speed to get over a jump, but I do need *energy* in my motor *before* I get to the jump, so that I can spring. This energy must be contained as we approach the obstacle at a steady, even, controlled pace, and you should sit and move exactly as you would at this gait and pace if there were no obstacle looming up in front of you.

As we near the obstacle, a few strides away, you will feel me getting ready for the TAKE-OFF, which is when we leave the ground in our spring. As I stretch my head and neck forward more and more and prepare to balance myself you must allow your hands to follow this balancing motion, with arms relaxed. This will release the energy which has been held back in my hindquarters during the approach and it will be ready to use in the spring which I must now make. As I leave the ground on the take-off, your shoulders and upper body must stay forward, with your hands following the balancing thrust of my head and neck. Your weight must be well forward on your thighs.

In the FLIGHT over the obstacle, your hands continue to follow the balancing needs of my forehand, your upper body moving accordingly.

On LANDING, I raise my head and neck as I return to my stride. Your body returns to the right position for the gait I am resuming; you maintain your contact and, as you ride me straight away from the obstacle, collect me again.

Practice first with rails upon the ground, several feet apart. I can walk or trot over these, without jumping. In this way you can perfect your approach without worrying about staying on and practice looking ahead rather than down at the rails as I step over them. You can also practice riding straight away from the rails.

Raise the rails gradually until I have to make a small spring over them. (These arrangements of rails at a low height are known as *cavaletti*.)

157

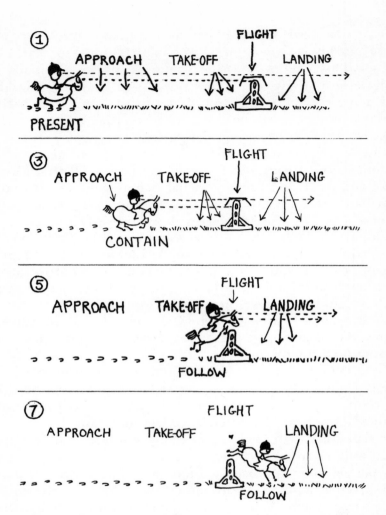

① **PRESENT**
APPROACH   TAKE-OFF   FLIGHT   LANDING

③ **CONTAIN**
APPROACH   TAKE-OFF   FLIGHT   LANDING

⑤ **FOLLOW**
APPROACH   TAKE-OFF   FLIGHT   LANDING

⑦ **FOLLOW**
APPROACH   TAKE-OFF   FLIGHT   LANDING

At first, until you are used to the sensation of jumping and can stay in balance with me, you should take a piece of my mane in your fingers to prevent you from pulling my mouth by accident, if you get "left behind."

158

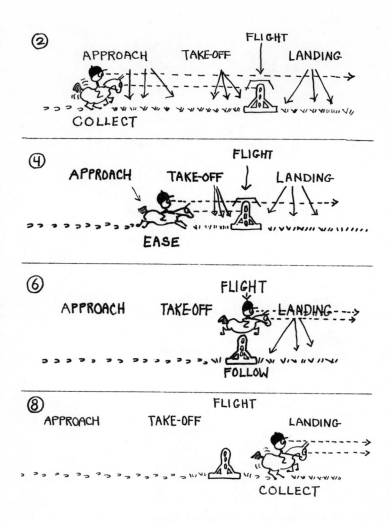

I can jump almost any small obstacle from a trot, which is a good gait for us to use in practicing. However, you will find it much easier to stay with me when I jump from a cantering stride. This stride moves naturally into the spring of a jump.

159

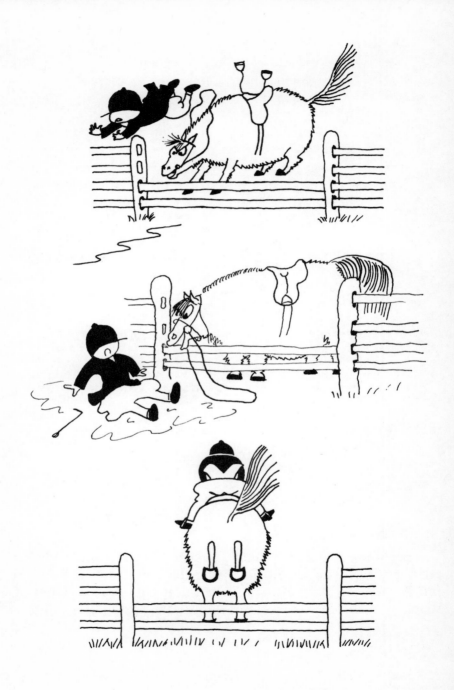

If you follow these steps in jumping, you will stay in control of me and be able to use your aids whenever needed. By moving with me up to the jump and following my motions over it, you will stay balanced and secure upon my back.

Here are some DON'TS to observe if you want our jumping to be a success. (Unfortunately, you will see many riders doing these very things, thinking that they are "riding a horse over a jump," but usually the poor horse is jumping in spite of their interference, not because of their assistance!)

Don't start sideways at a jump . . . I can't handle myself as well!

Don't look down during any part of the jump . . . it puts you (and therefore me) out of balance.

Don't race down to the obstacle . . . my energy will probably be wasted getting there—with none left for my spring!

Don't let me approach uncollected . . . with my head hanging down and my hocks out behind me, I am in no position to spring into the air!

Don't try to jump before we get there, by climbing out on my neck with your "tail feathers" up in the air! (This makes it impossible for you to control or assist me with your aids—to say nothing of burdening my neck and putting weight on my forehand just when it needs to be raised for take-off.) Just keep moving with my motions and you will be with me on the take-off!

161

Don't suddenly shoot your shoulders forward and thrust your arms up my neck, with contact gone and reins hanging loose, just as I am about to take-off . . . the change from strong contact to loose rein is enough to unbalance me completely! Give me freedom of my head and neck as I ask for it—don't anticipate!

Don't try to speed up my motor at the last minute, by banging my sides with flailing legs when we are right on top of the jump! It's too late by then if my motor is dead, and it just makes my balance worse. The time to put energy in my motor is before we approach the jump; then you can contain it in your hands until it is needed for the take-off. If you feel that I need encouragement at the last minute— apply pressure stronly with both legs—don't kick me!

Don't finish the jump before I do by dropping your weight on my back before I have completed my flight . . . this will make me drop my hindquarters on top of the jump! Keep your weight well forward on your thighs until I have taken at least one stride after landing. Remember, the jump is not completed until I have been re-collected, and ridden straight away from the obstacle!

Don't use a single obstacle over which to practice . . . both you and I will benefit more from jumping a series of obstacles. I will not become so bored, and will be less likely to become careless in my jumping. You must stay as alert and active when you are riding me from one jump to the next, as you are over the obstacle itself.

10. Fun That We Can Have Together, Now and Later On

When you are secure and steady on my back, and know how to use your aids well enough to be in control of me at all gaits in the ring in which we have been learning together, we are then ready to leave the enclosed area, and can start to enjoy many new experiences and pleasures.

By now we are fast friends who understand each other very well. You now know that if you use your aids properly, with the right amount of pressure at the correct time, I will respond promptly and follow your instructions. And I know that you will be in constant, comfortable communication with me, making me aware of your wishes kindly, quietly and clearly.

You will be able to anticipate and avoid (or calmly correct if necessary) any problems which arise in our relationship; and I will feel confident and secure in your sensible guidance.

This makes us real partners, ready to enjoy together the many activities and sports in which we can participate already, or for which we can prepare ourselves with further training and practice.

In the beginning while you were learning to control me at different gaits we did not venture very far from the ring. We did this so that you could return quickly to the confines of the ring for further practice if you were losing control of me.

So until now, all our riding has been done on ground that was smooth and level. Now we can start to leave this area and ride through woods and across fields, either on paths especially cleared for riding, called "bridle paths" or "trails," or by simply taking our own course "cross-country." (Sometimes we may ride on little-used dirt roads but we should always avoid, if possible, hard-surfaced roads with automobile traffic.)

In cross-country riding we will have to watch out for different conditions of the ground, and to take the precautions that are necessary to ride safely over or through them. These general conditions are known as the *footing* or the *going*.

The footing may be slippery; even good footing often becomes slippery when wet with rain. When wet going becomes frozen, it is *always* dangerous. (In winter the blacksmith will put sharp *caulks* on my shoes to give me a grip on icy ground.)

Some kinds of snow make slippery footing. Wet snow makes bad going, because the snow packs in balls in the sole of my hoof, making me walk on a slippery rolling surface. This is awkward for me, and is also a strain on my legs.

Dismount and knock the snow balls out of my hooves on such days. Ride carefully when I *ball up*.

Frozen ground is always a difficult surface for riding. Hoof-prints and ruts that were made when the going was muddy freeze solidly and may cause me to trip. Then the warmth of the sun may thaw the top few inches of the ground, and make it slippery. Hard-surfaced highways are always *dangerously* slippery for me with my metal shoes! *Don't ride on them!*

If you cannot avoid riding down a public road, keep well over on the gravel or dirt edge. Your extended arm *may* slow down an approaching automobile, but don't depend on any consideration from motorists. Few of them realize that a horse may be frightened by a speeding, noisy car. In some places the rule is for pedestrians, bicyclists and riders to ride facing on-coming traffic so that they can see what is coming. In other areas all traffic must stay on the right hand side.

If an automobile approaches from the rear—turn my head slightly toward it so I can see it approach from that side. Then if I shy I will jump away from it, and not in front of it! It is easier to keep me from swinging my hindquarters in front of an oncoming car if I am moving forward; so *keep me moving!* *Don't let me stop.*

Whenever the footing is slippery, keep a tight seat and ride me with some collection, with good, supporting contact. I need to keep my feet well under me and your assistance will steady me, particularly around corners or making turns.

The going will be called "heavy," and will be difficult for me to struggle through whenever the ground is holding water, for example, in swamps and bogs near streams, or in ploughed ground after a rainfall. If heavy going cannot be avoided, I should be ridden through it slowly, at a walk, on strong, supporting contact. Making me hurry or flounder through heavy going can easily injure my legs.

The going which we will encounter cross-country may be uneven and sometimes quite rough. I should be well collected when moving over rough going. Don't let me stumble, by riding me with a loose rein and with my forehand overweighted!

Never cross a field without keeping a watchful eye for any depression in the ground such as a ditch or gully, and especially for a ground hog hole. Stepping into a hole can give both of us a bad tumble.

Don't be surprised if I balk at crossing a stream the first time I see one. It may take some time and patience before I will try to cross it—and my first attempt may be a large leap to try to clear it! Hold onto my mane in this case so that you won't "ride" on my jaw. Also, don't forget that I will see many new sights, hear many new sounds and perhaps get some sudden surprises while we are riding cross-country. So always be ready to calm me, if necessary.

Another thing you must know, when you ride cross-country, is how to ride up and down grades of different heights. I should be ridden more slowly going downhill, and the steeper the incline, the slower the pace. Your seat should stay secure and I should have good supporting contact. Don't let my head hang down or I may stumble; collect me if necessary.

Going uphill, move your weight forward to free my hindquarters, so they can push us uphill.

Remember that I will tend to go faster downhill, and go slower uphill. If you want to keep a steady pace or cadence, you must begin to use your restraining aids before starting downhill and your driving aids before starting uphill.

When I am feeling full of pep or "frisky" it is a good idea to let me work off some of my high spirits by trotting or cantering uphill. I cannot put down my head and kick up my heels in play, or *buck,* as it is called, very easily when hill climbing. But be very careful riding me downhill when I am feeling frisky. (A buck on the downgrade can unseat you!) Keep a tight seat, hold my head up and control my actions!

In the summer when there has been little rainfall the ground becomes very dusty. Don't ride too close behind other horses and ponies or I will be forced to inhale the dust kicked up by their hooves. This is unpleasant and annoying to me and is so bad for my lungs that I may start coughing.

Do not ride *across* fields planted with crops; always ride *around* their edges.

Do not stir up cattle or sheep by galloping among them or near them. And never, never let the farmer's livestock escape from a field because you have carelessly forgotten to shut and latch a gate behind you, or have failed to replace a bar that you lowered in a gateway or fence.

(Later, when you are jumping fences, if you happen to crack or break a rail, you should repair it temporarily the best you can, and promptly report the damage to the owner of the fence so that he can quickly make the necessary repairs. The cost of this should really come out of your allowance, for it has been your fault!)

Never forget that the pleasure you enjoy in riding across-country is due to the hospitality of the owners of the property. Return their courtesy in full measure, and be a grateful guest wherever you ride.

As soon as you can safely ride cross-country, you are eligible to become a member of the UNITED STATES PONY CLUBS.

This is a national organization for young riders under twenty-one, whose objective is to teach riding, mounted sports and the care of horses and ponies. It was established in this country in 1953 and is patterned after the British Pony Club, a voluntary youth organization for those interested in ponies and riding, and is represented in no less than 21 countries with a total membership of almost 70,000. It is the largest association of riders in the world.

Branch Clubs are grouped into Regions, under the guidance of the *Supervisor* of each Region and the *District Commissioner* of the branch Pony Club.

With the assistance of experienced volunteer instructors, these Pony Club branches provide programs of mounted and unmounted instruction in horsemanship and horse management, group participation in mounted games and summer riding camp sessions, an introduction to the sport of Foxhunting if the branch is under the auspices of a Recognized Hunt Club, and to the fundamentals of the game of Polo if it is played in the area.

Competitions (known as *rallies*) are held in various phases of horsemanship and horse management, with selected Branch Club teams at different levels of progress competing with other Clubs within their Region. Then the winners vie with other winners for the National Championships.

The three mounted phases of rally competition are patterned after the three phases (Dressage, Cross-Country and Stadium Jumping) which make up the Olympic Three-Day competition, in which our own Three-Day team competes.

Thus if you dream of riding in the Olympic Games some day, one of the best ways of preparing yourself is to join the Pony Club. Several Pony Club graduates have already made our team!

FOXHUNTING is a mounted sport which you and I can start to enjoy after you have very good control over me through your aids, after we have learned how to ride successfully across country and after we know something about jumping obstacles.

The object of this sport is to find and pursue the fox, a very clever and elusive animal, who knows many cunning ways to outwit his pursuers. The chasing is done by hounds especially bred and trained to follow the fox's scent.

These *foxhounds* hunt in *packs* or groups. The whole hunt is managed by the *Master of Fox Hounds,* and the hounds are controlled by the *huntsman,* who is assisted by one or two *whippers-in* (called *"whips"* for short). The riders who are members of the Hunt are called the *field* and they follow behind the *Master*.

If you are lucky enough to be near a branch of the Pony Club which is sponsored by a hunt club, you will have a chance to be introduced to hunting as a guest of this club, at meets arranged especially for young riders. Before you participate in these hunts you will be taught, at unmounted Pony Club meetings, something of the history, traditions and customs of foxhunting, the manner in which it is conducted and the language and etiquette of the sport.

Some packs are privately owned, and hunting with them is at the invitation of the Master only. Other hunts which are supported by membership dues permit guests to join the day's hunting upon payment of a *capping fee*. If you are permitted to hunt with a local pack at other times than Pony Club meets, an experienced adult should accompany you.

Your first participation in foxhunting should be in the form of *hill-topping*, which means watching the course of the hunt from some point of vantage, but not mingling with the field. This way you can watch hounds work, and I can become used to the sight of many horses going very fast.

A mounted game which is great fun to play and also very exciting to watch is called POLO. It is played by two teams of four players each outdoors on turf playing fields, or by teams of three players in indoor arenas. The object of the game is to score a goal by driving a *ball* between the opponent's goal posts, using a *polo mallet* to strike the ball.

Polo is a very fast game, requiring speed and agility on the part of the *polo pony* and quick thinking and skill on the part of the *polo player*.

There are many *polo clubs* throughout the country, whose teams play against other local clubs and engage in *tournaments* with visiting teams from distant points. Some polo clubs have pre-season training programs in which young riders can learn the rudiments of the game, and many branches of the pony club now give basic instruction in polo to their members.

Polo is a game packed with action, in which skill in wielding a mallet must be combined with skill in horsemanship. While polo is usually a masculine sport, one of England's best polo players is a hard-riding lady! All young riders should learn the game if they have the opportunity. It will be fun for them, and for their ponies, too!

Another form of fun which we can have together is to compete in HORSE SHOWS. (Of course, both you and I should become quite expert before we attempt to enter any horse show competition, except in beginners' classes.)

There is an organization called the American Horse Shows Association, which governs all Recognized horse shows in the United States. Riders of all ages are eligible to join this association. *Member Shows* follow the rules set up by the Association and all *judges* at these shows must be certified by the AHSA.

Many horse shows are held just for junior exhibitors, while other hold classes especially for ponies and young riders.

In some classes the ability and form I show at my gaits or over obstacles is judged, called *Under Saddle, Hunter* and *Jumper* classes. There is also a division in which I am not considered, but only your skill in horsemanship is judged, called *Equitation* classes.

We should not enter any classes until we are certain that we are able to perform creditably and are adequately prepared. We will always strive to win by making the best possible appearance and performing to the best of our ability. But win or lose— we will always display the very best sportsmanship!

175

The highest goal for every young rider is to be able to represent our country in international competition as a member of the UNITED STATES EQUESTRIAN TEAM.

The USET includes a *Dressage* team, a *Three-day* team and a *Prix des Nations* team. A dressage team usually consists of three riders, while the other two teams have four. The excellence and obedience with which the horse performs a special program of movements in a small ring is judged in the dressage competition. In the three-day event, the horse does three different tests on three separate days. He performs a modified dressage test the first day, has an endurance trial and jumps a cross-country course on the second day, and finishes the last day by jumping a stadium jumping course. The Prix des Nations Team competes over extremely difficult, high and wide obstacles in an enclosed arena. Speed is often a factor as well as size of fences.

These teams compete annually in International Shows abroad, in preparation for the equestrian competition at the *Olympic Games,* in which the outstanding riders of the world compete every fourth year.

Our teams are supported solely by the contributions of riders of all ages. (You may become a Junior Member by writing USET, Gladstone, New Jersey.)

176

GETTING A HORSE OF YOUR OWN

When you first start to learn about horses and ponies—how to handle them on the ground and how to ride them—you should try to find a horse or pony (like me!) that has already had a lot of experience in teaching other boys and girls.

You don't want to start out with a young, inexperienced pony, who is just learning about things himself. The combination of a "green" (which means inexperienced) horse or pony and a green rider is usually unsuccessful, and it can be dangerous.

At first you probably will not have a pony of your own, but will want to seek the best possible place at which to ride and take your instruction. Such an establishment will have well qualified instructors, calm and patient horses and ponies to ride while you are learning, and a proper ring for beginners.

Tell the instructor that you are a beginner, and don't pretend to be more expert than you are. It is not brave or clever to attempt something for which you are not prepared, and it is simply foolhardy to try to ride a horse or pony that takes knowledge and experience to control if you don't have much of either!

If you are one of the very fortunate young riders whose parents have promised them a horse or pony of their own, there are some important things to consider first. You should discuss them carefully with your parents before they get you a horse.

AGE is important to consider. It takes at least five or six years of training and experience under all conditions for a pony to become a suitable mount for a beginner, so it is best to look for one at least a year older than this. (With proper care a pony will remain a safe and useful mount until he is well up in his teens, which would be getting elderly for a horse.) You will be much safer if you begin with a wise, old pony who prefers to go slowly while you are learning.

178

SOUNDNESS is important to consider. When I am *sound* it means that I am healthy, without any defects that might make me lame, affect my breathing or impair my vision.

An examination for soundness should be made by an animal doctor, who is a doctor of veterinary medicine, known as your *veterinarian* (or "vet," for short). Some veterinarians are called *equine practitioners* which means that they specialize in treating horses and ponies.

TEMPERAMENT is extremely important to consider. Horses and ponies vary, just like people, in their dispositions. Most are agreeable, pleasant and willing, but some are disagreeable, unpleasant and obstinate (usually because they have been mistreated or badly managed). Also, like people, some are much more nervous and high-strung than others. These may be good at racing, but they are not at all suitable as mounts when learning to ride! You want one with as calm and placid a disposition as possible.

CONFORMATION—the way I am made physically—is important to consider. Sometimes defects in conformation can make horses and ponies less safe to ride or more difficult to care for. Badly formed feet or legs can cause horses and ponies to trip and stumble; weak loins can cause fatigue while insufficient room for digestive organs can make it difficult to keep a horse or pony fat and healthy; a bad shoulder can make very rough gaits. A veterinarian's opinion should be consulted about possible faults in conformation.

GENERAL APPEARANCE should be the last consideration in the purchase of a horse or pony for a beginner. The color of your choice and a pretty outline will add to your pleasure in looking at your horse or pony, but will contribute nothing to either usefulness or safety. Horses and ponies come in so many breeds, colors, sizes and shapes that I'm sure you will find one that is exactly right for you.

Who knows? It might even be me!